Eva Schwarz

VISUAL PARANOIA

in *Rear Window, Blow-Up* and *The Truman Show*

ibidem-Verlag
Stuttgart

Bibliografische Information der Deutschen Nationalbibliothek
Die Deutsche Nationalbibliothek verzeichnet diese Publikation in der
Deutschen Nationalbibliografie; detaillierte bibliografische Daten sind im
Internet über http://dnb.d-nb.de abrufbar.

Bibliographic information published by the Deutsche Nationalbibliothek
Die Deutsche Nationalbibliothek lists this publication in the Deutsche Nationalbibliografie;
detailed bibliographic data are available in the Internet at http://dnb.d-nb.de.

Lektorat: Michael Gromm

Coverfoto: gagel

∞

Gedruckt auf alterungsbeständigem, säurefreien Papier
Printed on acid-free paper

ISBN-13: 978-3-89821-812-2

© *ibidem*-Verlag
Stuttgart 2011

Alle Rechte vorbehalten

Printed in Germany

Gratefully dedicated to those
who graciously helped and supported me
in manifold ways

CONTENT

PREFACE

With the present study, Eva Schwarz offers an exciting investigation of what has advanced in recent decades to an almost paradigmatic genre: films picturing and problematizing the growing society of surveillance. Her readings of Alfred Hitchcock's *Rear Window* (1954), Michelangelo Antonioni's *Blow-Up* (1966) and Peter Weir's *The Truman Show* (1998) are highly entertaining and accessible and, at the same time, a theoretically profound analysis of three milestones in cinematic history. This makes her book interesting for cineastes, academic audiences and paranoia aficionados, alike.

Starting with an in-depth discussion of recent cultural theories of postmodernism, she develops her concept of "visual paranoia". Paranoia, here understood in a non-clinical way, seems to be born out of an overall crisis of visual culture in postmodern society. The dominant regimen of images we encounter today in everyday life has far-reaching consequences for our general perception of reality: with the proliferation and ambiguity of images and signs in today's mass medial culture and a growing unreliability of images and their surfaces, scepticism, uncertainty and confusion have taken over.

In her first chapter, Schwarz outlines the generic development of the paranoia film by focussing her observations on the concept of the gaze and masterfully embedding them into a detailed interpretation of the three selected films. Taking her cue from the general theoretical framework of cultural paranoia, she explores three distinct ways of seeing, which exceed and outgrow mere cinematographic curiosity: scopophilic (Hitchcock), common photographic (Antonioni) and scopophobic paranoia (Weir).

In the chapter on *Rear Window*, Eva Schwarz discusses frames of self-reference and self-reflexivity and diagnoses movements within the film, which bear witness to an existential scepticism towards the act of seeing itself. The gaze as a substitute for (physical) movement seems to open up a space for a specific desire for knowledge, for a truth that is assumed to be lying behind the surface of phenomena. The protagonist's desire to accumulate information via visual perception entices him to suspect murder behind the scenes he observes and, finally, to doubt the reliability of the visible itself. Thus, Eva Schwarz argues, *Rear Window* seems to anticipate the postmodern crisis of the society of the spectacle.

In Antonioni's *Blow-Up*, visual scepticism seems to grow into a no-longer tangible complexity, openness and indefiniteness of all phenomena. According to what Schwarz calls "photographic paranoia", boundaries between reality and imagination in *Blow-Up* progressively blur in such a way that perception (the visible), representation (the image) and interpretation (assumption of murder) continuously seem to fold into one another. Here, paradoxically, the photograph serves as the medium that lends itself easily to an authentic mapping of reality and, at the same time, exposes the nature of powerful submission inherent in photography (Sontag).

Following in the same vein as *Rear Window*, *Blow-Up* tells the story of a crime, which is investigated thoroughly by the protagonist through the use of photographic methods. In this context, Eva Schwarz sketches another essential paradox characterising visual culture: with the magnification of the pictures, the signs relevant to the crime investigation become less visible and tenable. Visibility becomes a trap; the darkroom turns into a theatre where visual memory is relentlessly deconstructed. Schwarz's study elaborates in a detailed and knowledgeable way the profound transformation of images and their significance in this film: images become the only visual evidence of a murder, which – given the deep disbelief in visual culture – is doomed to remain ultimately unverifiable. The protagonist as a "postmodern voyeur" (Denzin) turns into a cipher, symbolizing the crisis of visual representation; a sign within a text narrating the mystery of the image.

The final chapter of Schwarz's book focuses on previous observations and enlarges upon the concept of "scopophobic paranoia", as depicted in *The Truman Show*. Here, the emphasis is less on the unreliability of images and texts, but rather on the production of meaning controlled and determined by an omnipresent media culture in postmodern society: hyper-realities and panopticism (Foucault), the disorientation felt by the protagonist (who ultimately personifies the percipient human subject in the media age) and hence his perambulations in an ambiguous parallel reality characterized by conspiracy and confusion. "Scopophobic paranoia" as a visual questioning of all that which is visible, eventually, gives rise to an unmasking of the simulacrum.

Eva Schwarz's study is impressing in its scope and depth of argumentation. It makes us aware of the panoptic regimen deeply inscribed in the postmodern society of the spectacle; a culture marked by the ubiquity of mass media and the visual. The author's thorough analysis raises fundamental questions about the control and power exerted by images and the regimen of the visual; questions that in the end leave the readers interrogating their own perception of reality.

Dr. Sabine Fries

Paraphrased and translated from German by Leyla Ercan

INTRODUCTION

> "Allowing us to know the way we see and have
> seen ourselves has been one of the greatest
> contributions of films to culture [...] one of the
> greatest achievements of film is its ability to
> open itself to cultural influences so directly."
>
> Leo Braudy, *The World in A Frame*, 180

Fredric Jameson describes films as cultural texts and socially symbolic acts that reflect the 'political unconscious' of a society. In this sense film expresses and influences the social and cultural trends of a respective period.[1]

In postmodern times this trend finds expression in a variety of paranoia films. Although films with paranoid plots already existed before, paranoia in film has gained increased proliferation throughout the last decades. The popularity of contemporary paranoia films reflects the emergence of 'cultural paranoia' as a condition of postmodern times.

Rooted in the 'paranoid style' of American politics and inspired by several events in the recent history of the United States, paranoia flourished and with it the number of conspiracy theories. Following the traumatic event of the Kennedy assassination in the 1960s, the rhetoric of conspiracy has been increasingly incorporated into common usage. Paranoia has become a widespread phenomenon that circulates through high and popular contemporary culture.

The culture of paranoia coincides with a culture that is dominated by the visual on the one hand and the 'postmodern condition', which is characterized by a loss of the real, on the other. Thus, paranoia not only expresses a general suspicion towards both authority and alleged truths, but also towards visual appearances. From this field of tension between seeing as believing and general scepticism towards the genuine nature of visual signs emerges visual paranoia. It reflects the assumption that appearances cannot be trusted. With a scrutinizing gaze, visual paranoia tries to discover the truth beyond the surface of reality.

In this study, I intend to investigate this kind of visual paranoia as it is represented in three relatively contemporary films: Alfred Hitchcock's *Rear*

---

[1] Douglas Kellner suggests a relationship between film and society in which "films take the raw material of social history and of social discourses and process them into products which are themselves historical events and social forces" as quoted in Ray Pratt, *Projecting Paranoia. Conspiratorial Visions in American Film* (Lawrence: Kansas University Press, 2001), 44

Window (1954), Michelangelo Antonioni's *Blow-Up* (1966) and a more recent film by Peter Weir, *The Truman Show* (1998).

I begin the first chapter of my book with a short survey of paranoia in film and the paranoia film. I will then demonstrate the significance of paranoia in postmodern culture by sketching the development from politically inspired paranoia towards cultural paranoia as all-pervasive phenomenon that permeates contemporary life. The chapter concludes with a description of how the strong implication of visuality in a postmodern context brings forth visual paranoia.

In the following three chapters I investigate different kinds of visual paranoia with reference to the three selected films. A discussion will follow the chronological order of the films' release.

In the chapter on *Rear Window*, visual paranoia appears in a scopophilic form. As the protagonist gathers visual evidence in the course of his voyeuristic observation of the neighbourhood he detects the hidden truth of a murder.

In the following chapter on *Blow-Up*, visual paranoia emerges as photographic paranoia, which also lures the protagonist into the investigation of a murder mystery. Since his photographic images turn out to be unreliable proof, however, the crime remains unsolved.

In the final chapter dealing with *The Truman Show*, visual paranoia finally takes the form of scopophobic paranoia. The protagonist gradually discovers that his entire existence has been manipulated. He finally manages to break the spell of the fake world he has been living in and escape.

Each chapter will be rounded off by a selection of stills from the films representatively reflecting the paranoid plot. With the assistance of the commenting captions the images aim at concatenating the bits and pieces and thus tracking the threads of the narratives of the respective film.

My conclusion contains a summary of the results of my analysis and a short demonstration of the development that can be traced through the chronology of the films' release.

I. THE CULTURE OF PARANOIA

1. Paranoia in film

Cinematic plots with paranoid tendencies are as old as cinema itself. Paranoia runs through cinematic history like a ghostly apparition. As Henry M. Taylor shows in his survey on the history of the paranoia film, the 'quasi-genre' or 'meta-genre' always needs another classical genre for support. Paranoia can be found as a latent element in the early expressionist film, in the pessimistic and dangerous atmospheres of the film noir as well as in science fiction and horror films. Many paranoia films are based on crime or political thrillers that 'explicitly' place paranoia in the foreground as a basic element, as they often deal with the detection of conspiracies.[2]

Most often the protagonists of paranoia films are figures whose work is of a cognitive, interpretive nature. They are detectives in film noir, or journalists, as in *All The President's Men*, or lawyers as in *JFK*.

Oscillating between realism and fantasy, the paranoia film often outlines a 'parallel world with alternative conditions'.[3] Its often sinister atmosphere is determined by a sense of mistrust, uncertainty and latent danger. The stylistic device of alienation is the filter often used to make reality visible from a different perspective. When the protagonists of paranoia films are suddenly drawn into situations that change their points of view, their former interpretations of their surrounding world begin to shift. Often, their realization turns into a real threat to their lives.

By drawing the spectator into a seemingly subjective perspective and making him perceive the cinematic reality from the protagonist's point of view, paranoia films 'filter' the (visual) information through the 'paranoid' protagonist, thus turning the spectator into a paranoid accomplice and investigator.[4]

As in most postmodern fiction, the final scenes of paranoia films often do not establish or re-establish normality, truth or peace. Using 'open closures' they keep 'the secret' by not declaring valid only one version of reality.[5]

---

[2] Henry M. Taylor, "Was bleibt ist das Kino. Ein Gespenst der Filmgeschichte: auf den Spuren des Paranoia-Films" in *Filmbulletin* 1 (2003), 47

[3] Taylor, 47

[4] Throughout the book I will use the masculine personal pronoun for the spectator. This is intended, however, to apply to the entire audience, both male and female.

[5] Taylor, 46-48. [Paul Auster's *City of Glass* and Thomas Pynchon's *The Crying of Lot 49* might serve as examples of literary fictions with 'open closures'.]

After the more vague and ominous paranoia of film noir, American culture of the 1950s was dominated by a paranoid strain aiming to promote and maintain a clear distinction between American identity and its potential enemies.[6] The American fear of totalitarian conformity through infiltration by communism and a latent anxiety about a Soviet nuclear attack found expression in many films about alien invasions or abductions, such as *Invasion from Mars* (1953) or *Invasion of the Body Snatchers* (1956). The language of physical invasion and germophobia gave expression to hysterical fears about all kinds of scapegoated others during the McCarthy years. Both functioned as a "figure for anxieties about attacks on the body politic and the failure of the national immune system".[7] This implied the latent danger of influences from within the nation, with women, blacks and homosexuals constituting a threat to what it means to be a 'straight' American citizen.

In 1962, *The Manchurian Candidate*, which was released one year before and thus anticipated the death of J.F. Kennedy, became 'the prototype' of political assassination thrillers.[8] It was followed by a wave of political thrillers during the 1970s, which were made under the influence of the political events and developments following the assassination of the American president. Films like *Klute* (1970), *The Parallax View* (1973), *The Conversation* (1973), *Three Days of the Condor* (1974) and *All the President's Men* (1976) were all inspired by the devastation of the people's trust in the national government.

After the great 1970s wave of political paranoia thrillers, following *JFK* (1991), which breathed new life into the suspicions about and speculations on the Kennedy assassination, paranoia has gained an obvious presence in many films in recent years.[9] A number of recent films with paranoid plots such as *Pi* (1997), *Conspiracy Theory* (1997), *Cube* (1998), *Arlington Road*

---

[6] Peter Knight, *Conspiracy Culture: From Kennedy to the X-Files* (London: Routledge, 2000), 174

[7] Knight, 169

[8] The anxiety of communist contamination is ironically incarnated in John Frankenheimer's *The Manchurian Candidate* (1962), in which the American government is infiltrated by Soviet spies in the disguise of conservative republicans, and an American Lieutenant is brain-washed and programmed to become an assassin. See Pratt, 91. (For further information on the film see also Greil Marcus, "A Dream of the Cold War: On *The Manchurian Candidate*" in *The Dustbin of History*, (Cambridge Massachusetts: Harvard University Press, 1995), 192-207

[9] Even thirty years later, the case became as much of topical interest as at the time of the Warren report, when Oliver Stone's version of the circumstances of the death of the American president aroused so much public turmoil that after the film *JFK* (1991) hitherto secret material concerning the case was finally disclosed to the public. Still today, people seem to be dreadfully fascinated by the case, the mystery of which has never been and probably never will be solved.

(1999) and *Memento* (2000) have successfully entertained the masses worldwide.

Ian Scott therefore sees in the 1990s "in actual fact a natural successor to the great paranoid film period of the 1970s".[10] Whereas several historical events have served the makers of films in the 1970s as material for many suspenseful political thrillers, Scott argues it is "the leap forward in technology [and] the extension of an observable culture that can perpetrate all our lives" that are the motivating factors for the new wave of contemporary paranoia films.[11] Scott also points out that contemporary paranoia films are much more abstract than those of former periods, as they are often concerned with "the power of media imagery and, ultimately, about film itself".[12] The subject of many recent paranoia films is therefore the loss of true authenticity in a world in which reality has become producible or reproducible, as for example in *The Game* (1997), *The Truman Show* (1998) and *The Matrix* (1999). Furthermore, technological development has also played an important part in redefining an enemy within Hollywood narratives in the contemporary era. Science fiction films such as *Blade Runner* (1982), *Total Recall* (1990), the *Terminator* series (1984/90/2003) and again *The Matrix* (1999) have constructed nightmare-like visions of a future world in which technology has become an uncontrollable force threatening the autonomy and independence of mankind.[13]

The promulgation of the end of all certainty through the popular 1990s U.S. television series *The X-Files* also shows that "paranoia is truly back in vogue".[14] FBI agents Mulder and Scully still deal with aliens and other mutant beings, yet they no longer represent the cold war paranoia, but rather the alienation of power, which, behind its democratic façade, has adopted totalitarian features.[15]

How can this cinematic trend be explained? Why is paranoia such a fascinating subject and successful ingredient of cinematic narratives? And why has it become so popular in recent years?

---

[10] Ian Scott, *American Politics in Hollywood Film* (Edinburgh: University Press, 2000), 103

[11] Scott, 103

[12] Jonathan Romney, "They're Out to Get You" in *The Guardian*, Media Section 19 October 1998, 6-7 (as quoted in Scott, 103)

[13] Scott, 103

[14] Scott, 102

[15] Andreas Balzer, "Der verdunkelte Horizont" in *Grimme. Zeitschrift für Programm, Forschung und Medienproduktion* No. 3 (1998), 52-53

The appearance of the 'cinema of paranoia' during the last decades reflects a cultural tendency in postmodern society - a phenomenon which has been termed cultural paranoia.[16]

2. Paranoid postmodernity

> "These are the paranoid years. Paranoia is not only fashionable, it's endemic. Nobody trusts or believes anybody any more and the resulting rot is doing more harm than speed."
>
> Ralph J. Gleason, *The Age of Paranoia* (1969), 424

> "Paranoia and conspiracy theories provide one way, at least, of knowing what is otherwise unknowable, of naming the anonymous yet unprecedentedly invasive system of institutional structures and communication networks."
>
> Peter and Will Brooker, *Postmodern After-Images*, 21

On cultural paranoia

Cultural paranoia is an expression that must be understood in a non-clinical sense. The term describes a cultural phenomenon. This involves a communication community or communicative system in which constructions of meaning and models of reality are permanently theorized on the ground of collective knowledge.[17] In this respect, cultural paranoia should be understood as trying to grasp a current tendency within contemporary society's modes of expression and communication in the context of the postmodern paradigm.

As Ray Pratt points out, in postmodernity "traditional distinctions between individual psychology on the one hand, and political and social philosophy on the other, have become obsolete".[18] Thus, the connection between paranoia and postmodernism is created by the fact that the conditions of both are characterized by a crisis in interpretation.[19] While clinical paranoia's positive regenerative effect as a reaction to a breakdown takes

---

[16] The term is used in publications of several authors. I refer, however, above all to Peter Knight's study on *Conspiracy Culture: From Kennedy to the X-Files* of 2000.

[17] Gerhard Bühler, *Postmoderne auf dem Bildschirm, auf der Leinwand: Musikvideos, Werbespots und David Lynchs 'Wild at Heart'* (St. Augustin: Gardez, 2002), 333

[18] Pratt (referring to Marcuse), 36

[19] Bran Nicol, "Reading Paranoia. Paranoia, Epistemophilia and the Postmodern Crisis of Interpretation" in *Literature and Psychology. A Journal of Psychoanalytic and Cultural Critics* 45, 1-2 (Nashville, Tennessee: MLA of America, 1999), 44

the form of an attempted reconstruction, cultural paranoia can be described as postmodern society's desire to make sense of and fathom reality in a time of crisis in epistemology, interpretation and representation.[20]

Cultural paranoia is an indication of cultural change; a cultural expression of human striving for coherence and of the attempt to understand and explain the continuity of human life in a time of change and loss of former norms and values. In postmodern times the human subject longs for the discovery that things are somehow connected "precisely because there is evidence all around that nothing is inherently connected".[21]

Conspiracy theory

Cultural paranoia finds expression in a heightened belief in conspiracy theories. Similar to the symptoms of psychological paranoia, delusions of grandeur and persecution complex, conspiracy theories are patterns of fixed belief, which persist even though social reality seems to contradict them. In this respect, cultural paranoia can be said to function according to Lacan's model of psychoses, as "an intensification of the projective dimension of knowledge, which involves imagining other perspectives [...] and thus [seeing] an alternative version to reality".[22]

Conspiracy theories perceive and interpret reality in new ways, and form an intrinsic whole that stands in opposition to common views or explanations. As the impossibility of grasping reality in its entirety results in the necessity of concentrating on fragments, conspiracy theories often move beyond prominent factors and bring forth unusual, sometimes exceptional versions explaining historical events or matters of daily life.

Conspiracy theories are based on the principle assumption that nothing can be taken for granted, that everything has a meaning and is somehow connected. This implies the hope or fear that "every seemingly insignificant fact or detail might turn out to be a clue to a larger plot, if only one could see the hidden connections".[23]

Generally, the stimulus of conspiracy theories lies in the human fascination with mysteries, or, as Daniel Pipes puts it: "Much conspiracism in the

---

[20] Freud and Lacan on paranoia as referred to in Oliver Keutzer, "Project Zweifel. Verdachtsmomente im Paranoia-Thriller" in *Kino der Extreme. Kulturanalytische Studien* (*Filmstudien Bd. 8*), ed. Marcus Stiglegger (St. Augustin: Gardez, 2002), 308

[21] Nicol, 47-48

[22] Lacan, *Fundamental; Psychoses* as quoted in Nicol, 46

[23] Knight, 204

United States is modish, reflecting a taste for puzzles and puzzlement."[24] There is the challenge of investigating like a detective and looking for clues, resembling a scientific process at the end of which there is the gratification of finally solving the mystery and maybe discovering a secret truth.

It is, however, a specifically postmodern pattern of thinking to create such theories. In a time in which human life is dominated by technology and information, and the view of the world is characterized by uncertainty and a lack of coherence, conspiracy theories are capable of transforming the world into a network of interconnected signs and meanings. Thus, by focusing on certain aspects and interpreting them as clues for an alternative view of the world, they offer the possibility to come to terms with an increasingly intricate and complex reality. Conspiracy in contemporary culture, as it were, "provides an everyday epistemological quick-fix to often intractably complex problems".[25] It provides the comfort of believing that everything is important and that it all makes sense.

Conspiracy culture

> "From below it is a popular movement within a population sensing it is being manipulated and controlled; from above it is a mind-set encouraged by national political leadership and the mass media."
>
> Ray Pratt, *Projecting Paranoia*, 9

Why has conspiracy thinking become so popular? Why has paranoia taken hold of postmodern society in this way?

The emergence of cultural paranoia as symptom of a postmodern way of feeling and thinking is closely related to the history of the United States, and has been influenced by several recent socio-political events and developments, which had a severely devastating effect on the American public. As Knight argues, cultural paranoia is rooted in a culture *of* and *about* conspiracy. As both phenomena are closely interlocked, Knight brings them together in the term 'conspiracy culture'. It might be argued that the culture *of* conspiracy, meaning conspiracy as mode of explanation, and the implicit mode of operation in US politics have inspired a culture *about* conspiracy.[26]

---

[24] Daniel Pipes, *Conspiracy. How the Paranoid Style Flourishes and Where It Comes from* (New York, London, Toronto, Sydney, Singapore: The Free Press, 1997), 14

[25] Knight, 8

[26] Knight, 3

From a culture *of* conspiracy towards a culture *about* conspiracy

> "A sceptical despair about the reality of
> politics and the institutions of our common
> social life - TV and newspapers - reinforces a
> sceptical despair about the progressive or
> conciliatory functions of art. The Nietzschean
> assumption that all such phenomena, from
> statements from the White House to everyday
> soap operas, are more or less secretly in the
> service of the maintenance of the power,
> economic and other, of somebody or other,
> rather than made in the service of any truth, is
> all-pervasive. It has led to a particularly
> paranoid strain in postmodernist theory and
> art, as well as in those popular films
> concerned with real or fictional conspiracies.
> How many people believe that Oliver Stone's
> film JFK [...] is not the fiction it is, but the
> truth?"
>
> Christopher Butler, *Postmodernism - A Very Short Introduction*, 112

As Richard Hofstadter points out in his essay "The Paranoid Style in American Politics", paranoia and conspiracy theories have a long tradition in US history. He describes how the exponents of this 'paranoid style' have not merely "see[n] conspiracies or plots here and there" but have regarded "conspiracy as the *motive force* in historical events".[27] The identity of the American nation is founded, as it were, on reasonable as well as irrational fears of real and imagined enemies.[28] Thus, political paranoia has, in the history of American politics, been a force that served the purpose of producing scapegoats and hatred, which was then turned against the respective 'hyped enemy'.

During the Cold War period, this 'paranoid force', which is representative of the culture *of* conspiracy, found expression in the exaggerated promotion of communism as a threatening force ready to subvert Western and, in particular, American democracy and culture. The US counteracted this hostile ideology through the Korean War (1950-53) and the Vietnam War (1964-73). The era was further characterized by the fear of nuclear warfare between the Soviet Union and the US, especially during the period of the Cuban missile crisis in 1962. Afraid that the nation might be infiltrated by

---

[27] Richard Hofstadter, *The Paranoid Style in American Politics and Other Essays* (New York: Alfred A. Knopf, 1965), 29. (Hofstadter has, however, also pointed out that this is not merely an American but also an international phenomenon. See Hofstadter, 6-7, 30)

[28] Knight, 2

communist spies, American politicians started FBI investigations under Senator McCarthy to search for the enemy, even among their own creative people, intellectuals and officials.[29]

The anti-communist wars and revelations about their doubtful motifs in particular, however, subtly called into question the legitimacy of the authority of the US in the world. In addition, the death of John F. Kennedy in 1963, one among several political assassinations during the period, caused a 'loss of innocence'.[30] Finally, revelations about the American government's involvement in conspiratorial activities such as the Watergate scandal provoked questions about the official versions of alleged truths or the reality of certain events. A general distrust towards the government and official agencies aroused increasing scepticism concerning authority. "Many Americans' sense of assured national and personal destiny has been cast into profound doubt".[31] How could a state be trusted when its representatives, members of the government, dodged its own rules? And how could, how should a democracy work like that?

Along with this loss of faith in the state's unimpeachability, the reduction of human autonomy through technology, social organizations and systems of communication has promoted a 'socio-psychological' landscape dominated by a general feeling of powerlessness. Timothy Melley terms this condition 'agency panic' and describes it as a "crisis in recent conceptions of personhood and human agency" in reaction to the postmodern concepts of fragmented, decentred subjectivity and constructed identity.[32] 'Agency panic' is characterized by an intense anxiety about the individual's loss of self-control and uncertainty about the efficacy and causes of individual human action. It expresses concern about limited access to information and the production of knowledge being manipulated by the mass media and controlled by an invisible authority.[33] Thus, 'agency panic' does not merely imply the fear of one's actions being controlled and of enforced conformity, but concern about whether the individual is in control of his or her own mind. In this respect, Melley identifies cultural paranoia as "cultural conversation about human autonomy and individuality".[34]

---

[29] Gérard Naziri, *Paranoia im amerikanischen Kino. Die 70er Jahre und die Folgen* (Filmstudien Vol. 35), (St. Augustin: Gardez, 2003), 19-23

[30] Knight, 23

[31] Knight, 4

[32] Timothy Melley, *Empire of Conspiracy: The Culture of Paranoia in Postwar America* (Ithaca New York and London: Cornell University Press, 2000), 14. (For 'agency panic' see Melley, 7-15)

[33] See Melley. 16

[34] Melley, 26

Finally, after fear and mistrust of a real existent enemy used as a scapegoat had turned into a diffuse threat from within the American nation, anxiety about being controlled and manipulated gave way to the more general assumption that there must be ubiquitous clandestine forces with conspiratorial power, which rule our increasingly interconnected globalized world. The suspicion against a concrete 'them' that works against an 'us' has increasingly turned into the notion of a conspiracy without conspirators.

This, however, also implies that the former "secure form of paranoia that bolstered one's sense of identity [... with ...] popular conspiracism [... turned into ...] a far more insecure version of conspiracy-infused anxiety, [...] a permanent uncertainty about fundamental issues of causality, agency, responsibility and identity".[35]

The 'primal scene' and the 'cultural turn' of paranoia

During the last couple of decades the language of conspiracy has not merely become a regular feature of American political discourse but also a familiar feature of cultural life. Especially since the time of the Kennedy assassination in 1963, which Knight describes as the 'primal scene', the phenomenon of paranoia has appeared on the stage of cultural history.[36] As president Kennedy was regarded as a personification of the national identity of American democracy, the events in Dallas caused, as it were, a national trauma. The nation gathered in front of its TV screens, watching the events surrounding and following the shooting, which were turned into an uninterrupted media-spectacle over several days. It was followed by an incessant investigation that involved endless repetition and re-interpretation of the 'visual evidence' provided by Abraham Zapruder's coincidental 8mm film material. All efforts to find the truth by means of this 'visual investigation' did not, however, result in knowledge but rather dissolved into confusion and uncertainty. The government's official version of the lone gunman Oswald could not explain the inconsistencies of the case, and it was not believed by wide sections of the American public. Even today, many Americans prefer to think that the murder was a result of a secret conspiracy against the president and his politics.

As a concomitant of the unsolved mystery of the Kennedy murder, an increased inclination for explaining things by means of conspiracy emerged. In this respect, the Kennedy assassination functions as an epistemological paradigm for the restless endeavour to find meaning in postmodern times.

---

[35] Knight, 4

[36] Knight, 4

Over the years, representations of the case by the media and popular culture have further contributed to this epistemological break.[37]

With its 'cultural turn', paranoia seems to have established itself among American society in such a significant way that conspiracy theories are no longer regarded as the "implausible visions of a lunatic fringe".[38] The 'paranoid style' no longer has mere political implications. There is a "significant shift in the function and format of conspiracy thinking [...] from the deliberate promotion of single-issue demonological doctrines to a more fluid and contradictory rhetoric of paranoia that suffuses everyday life and culture".[39] It has become a form of belief not only about socio-historical events but also about matters of daily life. Cultural paranoia inspires a different view of reality in general, and conspiracy theories have become many people's normal pattern of thinking about themselves and about what is happening in the world. Since paranoia has found good breeding ground in contemporary popular culture, and conspiracy theories have become a widespread subject in the media, the culture *of* conspiracy has finally engendered a culture *about* conspiracy.

Cultural paranoia refers to a critical/sceptical feeling among a society that has undergone social and cultural changes. It has induced in this society a sense of heightened awareness of the possibility of alternative realities or versions of truth. Throughout the last decades, postmodern existence has become "a continual process of trying to find meaning in the face of the knowledge that meaning is always relative and contingent".[40]

In postmodernity, every possible 'truth' may be opposed by its contrary. Therefore, plurality is the contemporary paradigm of the image of reality; the expectations of knowledge and action are marked by specification, difference and multidimensionality.[41] In this context, cultural paranoia provides a method of seeing multiple, interconnected stratifications of reality, since various versions of truth do not merely coexist unrelatedly but are also interconnected.[42]

---

[37] See Knight, 76-99

[38] Melley, vii

[39] Knight, 11

[40] Nicol, 46

[41] Wolfgang Welsch, ed., *Wege aus der Moderne. Schlüsseltexte der Postmoderne-Diskussion* (Berlin: Akademie, 1994), 13

[42] See Bühler (referring to Wolfgang Welsch), 40

According to the French philosopher Jean-François Lyotard (*The Postmodern Condition*, 1979) postmodernity is characterized by the end of grand narratives.[43] The underlying assumptions of ideas, concepts or systems formerly beyond question are no longer taken for granted and put under scrutiny. In this respect, conspiracy theories might be regarded as the alternative smaller narratives of the contemporary period. It might even be argued that conspiracy theory and paranoia act as 'master narratives' of postmodernity.[44]

3. Visual paranoia in visual culture

> "In this swirl of imagery, seeing is much more than believing. It is not just a part of everyday life, it is everyday life."
>
> Nicholas Mirzoeff, *An Introduction to Visual Culture*, 1

> "No culture has ever had this naïve and paranoiac, this puritanical and terrorist vision of signs."
>
> Jean Baudrillard in: *Postmodernism. A Reader*, 196

On visual culture

Postmodern paranoia coincides with a culture that is dominated by the visual. In fact, "postmodern culture is most postmodern when it is visual".[45] Contemporary life is replete with visual signs and images as postmodern society focuses on the visual to communicate, to create and to exchange meanings.

Due to the rise of audiovisual media and advanced technology, human experience and perception of reality have been increasingly visualized throughout the last century.[46] In accordance with this cultural change, contemporary life is to a great extent mediated through TV and film; work and leisure are centred on visual media. Even things that were formerly invisible to the human eye (and therefore difficult to fathom) are visualized

---

[43] John Hill, "Film and Postmodernsim" in *Encyclopedia of Postmodernism,* ed. Victor E. Taylor (London: Routledge, 2001), 96-97

[44] Melley, 8

[45] Nicholas Mirzoeff, *An Introduction to Visual Culture* (London and New York: Routledge, 1999), 3

[46] See also Martin Jay, "Scopic Regimes of Modernity" in *Vision and Visuality* (Dia Art Foundation, Discussions in Contemporary Culture No. 2), ed. Hal Foster (New York: The New Press, 1988/99), 3-4

by means of scientific imaging techniques such as X-ray and microscope. Advanced technologies enable transformation into visual patterns and computer images of that, which is not of a visual nature in the first place, like the activity of the brain or the heartbeat.[47]

In postmodern visual culture, audiovisual media dominates as a realm where a public notion of reality is created. Television, in particular, as 'window to the world', opens up a much wider field of mentally perceivable experience in a time of globalization. Norman K. Denzin therefore describes postmodernity as a cinematic age, which "knows itself through the reflections that flow from the camera's eye" and contemporary society as a cinematic society.[48] The French theorist Guy Debord also describes this phenomenon in his comments on what he named the 'society of the spectacle', concluding that the once directly lived experience has been increasingly replaced by representation.[49]

An additional aspect of the postmodern culture of visuality is constituted by the visual self-surveillance and self-control of its members by means of panopticism (especially 'panoptic' video surveillance systems).[50]

Visual culture in postmodern times is accompanied by a loss of the real. Debord points out that postmodern culture is characterized by a predominance of appearances.[51] Images increasingly leave the realm of representation and become independent from the real world. As a result,

---

[47] Mirzoeff, 1-6. See also Scott McQuire, *Visions of Modernity: Representation, Memory, Time and Space in the Age of the Camera* (London, Thousand Oaks and New Delhi: Sage Publications, 1998), 41

[48] Norman K. Denzin, *Images of Postmodern Society: Social Theory and Contemporary Cinema* (London, Newbury Park and New Delhi: Sage Publications, 1991), 155

[49] Guy Debord defined the 'society of the spectacle' in his publication of the same name (1967) by developing the term from the concept of the commodity as in the Communist Manifesto by Marx and Engels. Peter McGregor, 'The Truman Show' as a Study of 'the Society of the Spectacle' - Film As Text - Critical Essay, http://www.accessmylibrary.com/article-1G1-108551753/truman-show-study-society.html (14 August 2010). See also Anne Friedberg, *Window Shopping: Cinema and the Postmodern* (Berkeley, Los Angeles and Oxford: UCP, 1993), 178; and Guy Debord, *Die Gesellschaft des Spektakels* (Berlin: Klaus Bittermann, 1996), 13

[50] Michel Foucault describes the contemporary social system in terms of a panoptic order, in which disciplinary power is effected by the discriminating, inspective gaze. He refers to Jeremy Bentham's panopticon, a surveillance system with a panoptic architecture, as metaphor. See Ritvan Sentürk, *Postmoderne Tendenzen im Film* Dissertation, 1998 (Friedrich-Alexander-Universität Erlangen-Nürnberg, 1999), 42-43; and McQuire, 38-39. For Foucault's considerations concerning the panopticon see Michel Foucault, *Überwachen und Strafen* (Frankfurt am Main: Suhrkamp, 1976), 251-292

[51] Thomas Kleinspehn, *Der flüchtige Blick. Sehen und Identität in der Kultur der Neuzeit* (Reinbek bei Hamburg: Rowohlt, 1989), 320

the reality becomes distorted, or, as Jean Baudrillard would have it, the truth is concealed because the real is hidden behind signs and images. Baudrillard identifies simulation as the new image paradigm that replaces representation. He terms these visual signs simulacra. Appearing to be real, the simulacrum bears no reference to the real world. It is a mere visual surface lacking any depth of meaning.[52]

As in postmodernity, epistemological boundaries between simulations and reality are blurred, and it is increasingly difficult to distinguish between authentic and fake reality. Finally, signs and simulated images even seem to be more real than reality itself, and the former image of reality turns into a reality of the image.[53] Baudrillard terms this condition of the postmodern as 'hyperreality'.[54]

The postmodern crisis of interpretation therefore coincides with a crisis of the visual culture.[55] It is a crisis concerning what is real and how, and by whom reality, or the notion of it, is determined and authorized. It arises out of the tension between the idea that truth is self-evident on the surface appearance of things, on the one hand, and the assumption that truth might, however, be hidden somewhere beneath.

As a result, postmodernity's loss of sense regarding what is real raises general doubt about the true nature of visually perceived reality. With reference to the more general cultural paranoia I will continue by describing this specific phenomenon using the term 'visual paranoia'.

---

[52] Marita Sturken and Lisa Cartwright, *Practices of Looking: An Introduction to Visual Culture* (Oxford: University Press, 2001), 237

[53] See Bühler (referring to Siegfried J. Schmidt "Kulturelle Wirklichkeiten"), 333

[54] Sturken/Cartwright, 366

[55] Mirzoeff, 8

Visual paranoia

"The new paranoia [... has ...] less to do with
political anxieties, more to do with the feeling
that there is little verifiable reality in the
screen image itself, and by extension, in the
world we know through visual media. It's no
longer a question of who is to be trusted, as in
the Seventies, but a question of whether
anything, any image, any evidence of the state
of things, can be trusted."

Jonathan Romney, *The New Paranoia*, 39

"On the one hand, this shift to the visual
promotes a fascination with the image. On the
other hand, it produces an anxiety about the
potential power of images that has existed
since the time of Plato."

Sturken/Cartwright, *Practices of Looking*, 1

Visual paranoia is not primarily concerned with the truth about certain
socio-political or historical events. It is paranoia of an all-pervasive kind,
which is related to visual perception and reality in a time of visual crisis.

As the postmodern is characterized by a general doubt about visual
appearances, visual paranoia breaks the rules of conventional seeing. It
takes up a different perspective, which means that it does not take for
granted that seeing is believing, but always questions the credibility of
surface images. Although it still relies on visuality, visual paranoia deviates
from the 'normal' mode of seeing, turning it into a visual investigation.
With a scrutinizing gaze it examines the nature of the visually perceived. It
searches for hidden visible clues with the help of optical tools like
magnifying glasses or telephoto lenses. Visual paranoia considers the all-
pervasive possibility of another reality hidden somewhere beneath the
surface appearance of things.

In the following chapters I will investigate visual paranoia in three films
that were made in the last decades. Playing with the visual ambiguity of
reality, they are representative of a culture of the visual in a time of crisis.
With their plots revolving around visuality, they are concerned with their
protagonists' visual perception and notion of reality. Throughout the
narrations, things occur that make them change their perspective of
perception, and by gathering clues by means of visual investigation their
former view of reality begins to shift and they finally conclude with an
alternative interpretation.

In *Rear Window*, visual paranoia takes on the form of scopophilic voyeurism, which secretly observes visual evidence while searching for the hidden truth of a murder in the private sphere of the neighbourhood.

Visual paranoia in *Blow-Up* is also related to a crime. The focus on the visual is, however, linked to the photographic representation of reality. A series of photographs emerges as accidental evidence of an unexpected murderous scene in a public park.

The protagonists of *Rear Window* and *Blow-Up* are both voyeurs with a professional commitment who intrude into the private spheres of others. Here they discover that things are not how they expected them to be. With their suspicion aroused by slight inconsistencies in their perceived image of reality, both photographers detect traces of a crime. Turning detective, they "use their photographic skills to see more than the human eye is supposed to see" and finally become part of the spectacle they witness or have witnessed.[56] While Hitchcock's voyeur manages to fathom reality and prove the crime through panoptic observation of the suspected murderer, Antonioni's photographer learns that reality eludes his attempts to capture it – both as photographic representation on film and as definitive interpretation and verification of the crime.

Visual paranoia in *The Truman Show* has a twofold dimension. The protagonist of the film does not merely discover the ambiguous nature of a fragment of reality but that his entire existence is based on a fake reality. Moreover, he discovers that he is, as it were, visually persecuted by a secret panoptic video surveillance system and the voyeuristic gaze of a worldwide TV audience.

All three films involve the spectator by actively placing the interpretive investigative processes experienced by their protagonists on both the diegetic and the meta-diegetic level in the foreground.

As *Rear Window* and *Blow-Up* are extraordinary 'visual' films with less dialogue than usual, their narrative structures reflect their plots, focusing on visuality in general and on the visual and interpretive activities of their protagonists in particular. By establishing an identification of the camera's gaze with the protagonists' subjective view, the spectator is drawn into the process of their investigation and interpretation on the one hand, while on the other he simultaneously reflects upon the cinematic situation through self-reflexion, thus putting into perspective the subjective perception of the protagonist. The confusing and merging of realities establish a meta-level of reality that induces a sense of the ambiguous character of reality in the viewer and the relativity of any interpretation.

---

[56] Norman K. Denzin, *The Cinematic Society. The Voyeur's Gaze* (London, Thousand Oaks, New Delhi: Sage Publications, 1995), 155

27

In *The Truman Show*, the spectator's perception is not immersed in the protagonist's point of view. Instead, the audience is made to share the perspective of an on-screen audience, by which it is also mirrored in the narrative. In contrast to the other films, the visual paranoia of the protagonist is therefore observed more from the outside. The narrative structure of *The Truman Show* also enables the spectator to glimpse behind the scenes, thus providing him with a multidimensional perspective. Here again, the film's self-reflexiveness visualizes reality from different angles, and also contemplates visual perception in general and the voyeuristic/cinematic gaze in particular.

II. Scopophilic Paranoia in *Rear Window*

1. A narration of scopophilia and paranoia

"In his films Hitchcock reveals that behind
everyday reality there is another reality."

Juhani Pallasmaa, *The Architecture of Image*, 174

Based on the short story *It Had to Be Murder* by Cornell Woolrich, the plot of Alfred Hitchcock's *Rear Window* (1954) revolves around murder. The film narrates a crime story in an unconventional way, however, as it neither contains a crime scene nor images revealing a view of the corpse of the murdered woman. Convinced that he witnessed evidence of a crime, the protagonist of the film traces and detects a secret murder in the neighbourhood across the courtyard by means of 'visual investigation'. Just as "the terror is not in the scene projected on the screen, but in the minds of the audience", the murder develops within Jeffries's logic of interpretation.[57]

As I have already mentioned, *Rear Window* is a film of an exceptionally visual nature. Approximately one third of the entire duration of the film is made up of silent images, most of which are composed of the protagonist's observations (that is, 'subjective shots' from Jeffries's point of view).[58] The plot's focus on visuality is thus reflected by the narrative's 'film within film' structure.

In this self-reflexive structure, the protagonist is the most crucial element. He is the 'pivotal point' that connects the different levels of the narrative. These levels are separated, as it were, by Jeffries's rear window. The scenes behind the window, inside the flat, where the narrative follows the protagonist's private life with his girlfriend, and the daily visits by the nurse constitute the frame for the film in the film. In the other film, the protagonist mainly functions as an onlooker. As he gazes out of his rear window and observes the action framed by the windows of the building

---

[57] Juhani Pallasmaa, *The Architecture of Image. Existential Space in Cinema* (Helsinki: Rakennustieto, 2001), 156

[58] The strong focus on visuality is sustained by the film's renouncement of off-screen music. There are merely the sounds from the street (and the tenants), music and voices from someone's radio as well as music from the composer who is part of Jeffries observations (and thus the spectacle). Moreover, this renouncement also sustains the spectator's identification with the protagonist. Without a score, the audience merely shares Jeffries's auditory impressions. Thus, the film is not so much perceived as a cinematic fiction, but seems to be more 'real'.

opposite and what happens within, the window frames across the courtyard reveal the unfolding second narrative.[59]

At the end of *Rear Window*, the two levels of the film merge and the onlooker finally becomes part of the spectacle he has been watching. The film's sense of an ambiguous reality is thus rooted in the dual character of its protagonist as main character of the film - the photographer in his flat - on the one hand, and voyeur-spectator and first person narrator of what happens across the courtyard, on the other.

Narrative perspective

The scopophilic drive is an essential part of watching a film.[60] Scopophilia, a term which is derived from psychoanalysis, describes the human drive to look and the general pleasure in looking.[61] Moreover, the cinematic situation also implies an allusion to the voyeuristic practice of looking.[62] Yet the narrative structure of *Rear Window* turns the spectator into a voyeur in a dual sense.

The main part of the film's narrative is constituted by Jeffries's voyeuristic activities, or rather what he observes. Resembling the protagonist's view from the opposite side, most of the scenes are shot from his rear window. Most of these shots are, furthermore, enacted by a subjective camera that represents the protagonist's point of view. The subjectivity of this "second-hand voyeurism" creates in the spectator a feeling of being enclosed within the limited space of Jeffries's flat.[63] Moreover, the spectator's perspective

---

[59] Pallasmaa points out the opposition between the two spheres by referring to them as theatrical (inside the flat: more realistic and with dialogue) and cinematic (purely cinematic resembling silent film) sphere. Pallasmaa, 161

[60] As Christian Metz points out "The practice of the cinema is only possible through the perceptual passions: the desire to see (= scopic drive, scopophilia, voyeurism), which was alone engaged in the art of silent film [...]". Christian Metz, "The Imaginary Signifier" in *Film Theory and Criticism. Introductory Readings*, eds. Leo Braudy and Marshall Cohen (New York and Oxford: Oxford University Press, 1999), 808

[61] Scopophobia lacks the sexual/erotic implication inherent in the term voyeurism that is defined as the pleasure of (male) looking (at women) without being seen. See Sturken/Cartwright, 365

[62] As Laura Mulvey points out, cinema does not merely satisfy "a primordial wish for pleasurable looking" but through its conditions of screening and narrative conventions it gives "the spectator an illusion of looking into a private world", thus promoting an "illusion of voyeuristic separation" and "playing on their voyeuristic phantasy". Laura Mulvey, "Visual Pleasure and Narrative Cinema" in *Film Theory and Criticism. Introductory Readings*, eds. Leo Braudy and Marshall Cohen (New York and Oxford: Oxford University Press, 1999), 842

[63] Sharff, 179

is merged into Jeffries's voyeuristic gaze. As a result, the film within the film is experienced as through the protagonist's eyes.[64]

This 'filtering' of the audience's visual perception through Jeffries's consciousness not only turns the spectator into an accomplice in voyeurism but also draws him into participating in the process of investigation and interpretation from the protagonist's perspective.

Despite his almost complete identification with Jeffries, however, the spectator adopts a split perspective in his perception/reception of the film. The audience's gaze is able, as it were, to penetrate the protagonist's rear window in both directions, so that their visual field also includes the narrative sphere inside Jeffries's flat and, thus, the frame of the plot that unfolds therein. Although the film is mostly perceived from the protagonist's point of view, the perspective of the spectator's voyeurism also contains the voyeur and his voyeuristic activity. [65]

This superior position also enables the spectator to see what happens across the yard whenever Jeffries is not looking; for example when he is asleep or immersed in a kiss with his girlfriend. The audience, therefore, is provided with a piece of visual information that the protagonist misses: the lady in black, who might have been an important detail for his investigation.[66] This knowing a little bit more than Jeffries, as it were, strengthens the spectator's position as 'meta-voyeur'.

The spectator as voyeur

The gap left between Jeffries's consciousness and the spectator creates what Stefan Sharff describes as a "complex dichotomy between two modes of perception".[67] On the one hand, the protagonist functions as a medium for the audience. In sharing Jeffries's gaze, the spectator sees what the protagonist perceives. As the audience, however, also observes the voyeur

---

[64] Wood, 65

[65] Accordingly, the spectator's interpretation is also determined by the protagonist's (and his assistants') reactions to their observations. Watching Jeffries pondering on what he has seen adds to the audience's visual information and influences their interpretation of the 'shared' voyeuristic observations.

[66] Although the camera pan is experienced as if it represents the protagonist's subjective point of view, it includes frames of the sleeping Jeffries at the beginning and end. This device has been termed 'autonomous' camera by Ned Rifkin in *Antonioni's Visual Language* (Ann Arbor, MI: UNI Research Press, 1982) 106. Brigitte Desalm describes this as 'conspiratorial behaviour' (my translation). Brigitte Desalm, "Überwachen und Strafen - Einiges über die Blicke bei Hitchcock" in *Alfred Hitchcock*, eds. Lars-Olav Beier and Georg Seeßlen (Berlin: Bertz, 1999), 42

[67] Stefan Sharff, *The Art of Looking in Hitchcock's Rear Window* (New York: Limelight Editions 1997), 179. See also Wood, 65

as he watches, Jeffries, on the other hand, functions as a stand-in for the spectator. Seated immobilized in a dark room, confronted with a spectacle, Jeffries's spectatorship resembles the cinematic situation.[68] The rear window of his flat functions as a screen and what he observes through it resembles a silent film.[69] In this film's narrative, the murder story, with Thorwald as the protagonist, constitutes the main plot, while the episodes involving the other tenants, by whom Jeffries is sometimes lured away, are the subplots. Just as the film camera frames the narrative action for the viewer of Hitchcock's film, the windows of the building opposite frame the action Jeffries observes. In both cases the frame determines and restricts what will be seen and known.[70]

Thus, through its self-reflexivity *Rear Window* demonstrates the principles underlying cinematic perception. The film reflects within its diegetic content its own process of enunciation and consumption.[71] Its convoluted narrative structure induces a sense of ambiguity or dual reality in the viewer, which is sustained by the direction of the gaze through the rear window, as it suggests (as does also the title of the film) that what is to be observed might be of an equivocal nature.[72]

Introduction of the cinematic gaze as visual investigation

During the first few minutes of *Rear Window* the audience becomes familiar with the narrative situation of the film. The exposition introduces the cinematic gaze as visual investigation before the voyeuristic perspective

---

[68] The significance of *Rear* Window as a metaphor for cinema or as a study in film making and viewing is elaborated on in almost every publication on the film. See Denzin, *Cinematic Society*, 120. Sturken/Cartwright, 77. Pallasmaa, 154

[69] Or it might rather be argued that the windows resemble a set of 8mm film screens and the rear window of Jeffries flat resembles a "giant eye". (Miran Bozovic describes Jeffries as a man who is entrapped within his own eye. Miran Bozovic, "The Man Behind His Own Retina" in *Everything You Always Wanted to Know about Lacan (but were Afraid to Ask Hitchcock)*, ed. Slavoj Zizek (London, New York: Verso, 1992), 161-164

[70] Sturken/Cartwright, 78

[71] Zizek describes this as quite a postmodernist feature of the film. Slavoj Zizek, "Alfred Hitchcock, or, The Form and its Historical Mediation" in *Everything You Always Wanted to Know about Lacan (but were Afraid to Ask Hitchcock)*, ed. Slavoj Zizek (London, New York: Verso, 1992), 5

[72] Martine Lerude-Flechet, "Schauspiel des Blicks" in *Das unbewusste Sehen: Texte zu Psychoanalyse, Film, Kino*. Gesellschaft für Filmtheorie, eds. August Ruhs et al. (Wien: Löcker, 1989), 103; Denzin, *Cinematic Society*, 121

(and the interpretation from Jeffries's point of view) is established by the protagonist's viewing activities. It is a moment of 'pure looking'.[73]

After the bamboo blinds of Jeffries's rear window have risen underneath the opening titles, an 'autonomous' camera performs three circular pans around the courtyard and the interior of the protagonist's flat.[74] The pans around the courtyard introduce the sphere of the film within the film: the view unto the building opposite Jeffries's flat - as seen from his rear window. As the camera travels along, it acquaints the audience with some of the tenants who will be the objects of voyeuristic observation throughout the film. The second pan around Jeffries's flat provides a brief 'visual biography' of the protagonist.[75] Discovering Jeffries's broken leg in plaster, on which his name is inscribed, as well as photographic equipment and pictures, the camera floats around the room informing us about the protagonist's profession and the condition he is in.

Sharff has described these camera movements, which are repeatedly used throughout the film, as slow and surprise disclosure.[76] Both devices focus the audience's attention on the visual, as the camera's slow movements gradually provide the audience with information. And when these movements focus on an unexpected sight, this further encourages a perceptive mode of latent expectation that unpredictable yet significant details might be discovered here.[77]

Thus, from the very beginning, the spectator's perception of the film is structured by the underlying principle of the protagonist's investigation: watching means gathering visual information. Throughout the film the

---

[73] Brigitte Desalm, "Überwachen und Strafen - Einiges über die Blicke bei Hitchcock" (*Alfred Hitchcock*), 42. (It seems as if the 'voyeur-director' is still relaxing while the audience visits the set and takes a look around.)

[74] The raising of the blinds at the beginning of *Rear Window* alludes to the film as a staged play. Resembling a curtain covering the cinema screen or theatre stage, the blinds suggest to the viewer a secret visual world. The curtain is a symbol that evokes curiosity and suspense. As partition between the imaginary sphere and the real world it also indicates the illusion. Christine Noll Brinckmann, "Die filmische Urszene und der Film. Die Urszene" in *Das unbewusste Sehen: Texte zu Psychoanalyse, Film, Kino*. Gesellschaft für Filmtheorie, eds. August Ruhs et al. (Wien: Löcker, 1989), 26-28. (See also Pallasmaa, 158; and Miran Bozovic, "The Man Behind His Own Retina" (*Everything You Always Wanted to Know about Lacan*), 164

[75] Sharff, 8

[76] Sharff, 10, 22-25

[77] Sharff describes the surprise discovery of the sleeping Jeffries at the end of the pan around the courtyard as a 'lesson in seeing'. Despite the seemingly subjective perspective of the camera movement the spectator's expectation that he is looking with the protagonist is disappointed. As a result the audience's awareness will be sharpened for the following more detailed pan. See Sharff, 22

images perceived by the spectator will converge and gradually constitute in his mind visual knowledge, parallel to Jeffries's visual investigation, in the course of which his 'paranoid suspicion' turns into detection and the verification of a real crime.[78]

2. Scopophilic voyeurism

The photographer-voyeur

The protagonist of the film, L.B. Jeffries, is a professional photo-journalist. He is confined to a wheel chair with a broken leg having had an accident on his last assignment. Being a reckless adventurer, he desperately wants to return to work. Forced to stay at home, however, he finds himself in a "spiritual deadlock".[79]

Left to rely on himself, and confined to his flat, Jeffries's only connection to the world outside is his view from his rear window, as his flat faces onto the courtyard of the blocks of flats where he lives. Staring through his window, his wandering gaze functions as compensation for his immobilized body. Jeffries's "immobility eliminates the physicality and tactility of experience and transforms it into something purely visual; the eye subjects the other senses".[80]

Thus "reduced to a being of the gaze", he watches the people in the opposite building. He observes them in the courtyard or inside their flats through the frames of their open windows.[81] The courtyard resembles a stage and the entire content of the windows a 'scenic mosaic' of urban life.[82] It is a "world of dramaturgical appearances [in which] people are what they appear to be": the sexy blonde dancer surrounded by a swarm of adoring men, the young married couple spending most of their time in bed, the 'lonely heart' desperately trying to get some affection, the couple sleeping on their balcony and their little dog, the woman artist, the unhappy musician who has got stuck in composing a sad song and the

---

[78] For the film's introduction see also Helmut Merker, "Rear Window" (*Alfred Hitchcock*), 364-366

[79] Wood, 63

[80] Pallasmaa, 160

[81] Mladen Dolar, "A Father Who Is Not Quite Dead" in *Everything You Always Wanted to Know about Lacan (but were Afraid to Ask Hitchcock)*, ed. Slavoj Zizek (London, New York: Verso, 1992), 143

[82] Helmut Merker, "Rear Window" in *Alfred Hitchcock*, eds. Lars-Olav Beier and Georg Seeßlen (Berlin: Bertz, 1999), 364

salesman for costume jewellery named Lars Thorwald with his indisposed wife.[83]

Peeping on his neighbours, their little human troubles and tragedies are the visual entertainment of Jeffries's idle days.[84] The 'show' begins in the morning when the blinds rise as at the beginning of the film and it ends when his girlfriend Lisa lowers them in the evening, commenting it with the words that the show was over.[85]

Both his nurse and his girlfriend tell him, half-amused and half-concerned, to stop peeping. They are afraid of trouble. Jeffries, however, does not care about their well-meant warnings.

Jeffries's voyeurism is not the compulsive act of a pervert.[86] He merely tries to distract himself by indulging in his scopophilia. The perversion of his voyeurism lies mainly in the confusion of "the ontology of the window [...] as the inside is always definitely somebody's territory [and] as the object is [not] conscious of being under external scrutiny".[87]

Jeffries's gaze is, however, not merely inspired by curiosity out of boredom, but by a general lust to detect something. As a sensation-seeking photo-journalist he is, as it were, a voyeur by profession. In his job he is always looking for spectacular events and it is also not unusual for him to nose into other people's business.

Due to the limited space of the protagonist's flat and the restricted view across the courtyard, his usual boldness is transformed into an eager gaze.

---

[83] Denzin, *Cinematic Society*, 119. Concerning what Jeffries 'views' on/through the film screen windows, Helmut Merker mentions that the action that unfolds on the several window-screens (and in the flats behind them) belong to various different film genres like comedy, fairy tale, love story, crime thriller, melodrama and farce. Helmut Merker, "Rear Window" (*Alfred Hitchcock*), 369

[84] In this respect the protagonist resembles, as I have mentioned before, a spectator watching a film or, more contemporary, a person with his television on all day long who zaps through the channels with the volume turned down.

[85] His girlfriend Lisa also seems to be an object merely to be gazed at. The embodiment of a beautiful woman, her evening visits resemble the performance of a mannequin. Putting on the lights one by one she opens the show that is going on inside Jeffries's flat. (Wood, 66.) Towards the end of the film, when Lisa enters the sphere of the spectacle, she also becomes the heroine of his visual narrative.

[86] The protagonist's voyeurism is actually not primarily related to his male gaze watching female bodies, except for the erotic pleasure he might gain from the sexy blonde 'Miss Torso'.

[87] Pallasmaa, 169

Zizek, therefore, identifies Jeffries as one of Hitchcock's figures who typically see the more the less they observe.[88]

With his perception sharpened by his condition, and influenced by his desire for a (visual) thrill, the protagonist's scopophilia implies pleasure in looking both as entertainment and as the desire for knowledge. In the course of his observations his visual perceptions gradually develop into the paranoid suspicion of murder.

"There must be something wrong..." - How suspicion arises

Since he has been observing his neighbours for a few weeks, Jeffries knows what is going on in the neighbourhood. His general observation of the courtyard contributes to his amusement, but the tenants of the building across the courtyard do not arouse his deeper interest until, one night, he stumbles across something that captures his attention almost by accident.

Due to a summer heat wave Jeffries has fallen asleep in his wheel chair in front of his open rear window. Late at night he is woken by heavy rain. He is surprised to see the salesman from the building opposite leaving the house in rain gear with his samples case. Jeffries wonders what the man is up to at this late hour, and why he is leaving his sick wife alone in the flat. The observation arouses the voyeur-journalist's interest and he spends some time peering around the courtyard.

During the hours that follow Jeffries observes the salesman and his comings and goings: after returning home he later leaves again on two occasions, despite the stormy weather, and always carrying his aluminium case.

In the time between Thorwald's arrivals and departures Jeffries frequently falls asleep, only to wake up again to observe the next significant incident. In the morning, however, the 'hobby' detective becomes a victim of 'blundering by sleeping' and so misses Thorwald leaving the house accompanied by a woman dressed in black - a detail that would probably have become important evidence in his future investigation.[89]

---

[88] Stojan Pelko, "Punctum Caecum, or, Of Insight and Blindness" in *Everything You Always Wanted to Know about Lacan (but were Afraid to Ask Hitchcock)*, ed. Slavoj Zizek (London, New York: Verso, 1992), 111

[89] Sharff, 45

3. The voyeur turns detective

The salesman's mysterious nocturnal dealings arouse Jeffries's mistrust and suspicion. He wants to know what the man has transported in his samples case in the middle of the night - probably with the intention of remaining unnoticed. Assuming that there might be more to this than meets the eye, Jeffries's casual scopophilia turns into committed observation of the salesman.

Since Jeffries's investigative activity is restricted to his visual perception, however, he supports and improves it by using his binoculars and the telephoto lens of his camera. The 'portable keyholes' simultaneously increase the voyeuristic character of his observation and enable his scrutinizing gaze to get closer to his object of interest in order to see more. Like a detective, Jeffries searches for details that might give him a clue and explain the salesman's strange behaviour.

Observation of Thorwald's further activities increases Jeffries's mistrust. With the help of his optical tools the protagonist first watches the salesman cleaning his samples case and putting jewellery back into it, and, some time later, wrapping up a large knife and a saw in newspaper. Jeffries also notices that the blinds on Mrs Thorwald's bedroom window are down and that, contrary to his customary behaviour, the salesman does not appear to be caring for the woman all day long. What he has observed up to this point causes Jeffries to assume that something evil must have happened.

When the blinds on Mrs Thorwald's bedroom are finally pulled up again the next day, a further clue is exposed to Jeffries's gaze: the bedridden woman has disappeared out of her bed and, seemingly, out of the flat, too. Furthermore, Jeffries watches Thorwald tying up a big trunk with a rope, which is taken away by a transport company soon after. From now on, Jeffries believes that he has witnessed evidence of a crime. In his interpretation the visual information he has gathered adds up to the suspicion that the salesman must have murdered his wife.

The voyeur as paranoiac

Despite his obsession with the feeling that he has witnessed a murder, Jeffries did not observe a murderous scene. His suspicion emerges from his interpretation of the assumed visual evidence.[90]

---

[90] In this respect Jeffries's situation is similar to that of the photographer in *Blow-Up*. Although Antonioni's photographer was present when the crime happened, he is also not a direct eye-witness. He only discovers it later on his photographic images. On returning to the scene, however, he finds the corpse still lying in the park.

Seeking verification for his suspicion, Jeffries needs someone to help him. He therefore calls Tom Doyle, a detective friend of his, and puts him onto the case, providing him with his visual knowledge.

The New York detective undertakes investigations concerning the salesman and his wife. Doyle's findings, however, seem to dispel the assumption of murder, since he discovers that Mrs Thorwald merely seems to have gone away on holiday. Both the caretaker and neighbours claim to have seen the salesman taking his wife to the railway station early the previous morning. The detective even fishes out a postcard of from Thorwalds' letterbox, in which the wife tells her husband that she has arrived safely at her destination and that all is well.

Although the results of Doyle's investigative efforts seem sufficient to explain Mrs Thorwald's disappearance, they do not satisfy Jeffries. Besides his disappointment concerning his probable misinterpretation, the information delivered by the professional detective does not seem to correspond to his own visual knowledge of the case. If what the detective has told him sounds plausible with regard to the sudden departure of the salesman's wife, it does not, however, seem to explain the man's strange behaviour during the stormy night and the following day - the events that finally lured Jeffries onto the track of this mysterious case.

In countering Doyle's 'rational facts' with his own intuition and visual knowledge, the voyeur's epistemology is unravelled.[91] Since Jeffries does not believe that what he has observed is merely a series of coincidences, visual paranoia leaves him doubting the reliability of Doyle's information. Jeffries senses that there might be a secret truth hidden beyond the 'official version' attested by the professional detective and his arguments against murder.

The voyeur in the panoptic cinema

Doyle's employment having failed to confirm his suspicion, Jeffries dedicates himself to solving the mystery of this visual puzzle. As his observation investigation increasingly focuses on the target of his suspicion, the duality of Jeffries's voyeuristic gaze simultaneously implies both spectacle and surveillance.[92]

Jeffries's voyeurism does not merely work as a metaphor for cinema spectatorship, but also reflects a panoptic situation. Seated almost invisibly in the dark of his flat, Jeffries resembles a guard in the panoptic tower of Bentham's panopticon, as described by Michel Foucault. His inspecting gaze 'controls' the residents of the building across the courtyard. Separated by

---

[91] Denzin, *Cinematic Society*, 203

[92] Pallasmaa, 164

their window frames, they resemble the solitary individuals in the panoptic prison. When the lights are lit inside their 'flat-cells' at night they are exposed particularly to Jeffries's scrutinizing gaze through the frames of their open windows.[93]

With Jeffries's flat as a 'panoptic cinema', the 'quasi-panoptic' situation in *Rear Window* appears to be a forerunner to the video surveillance system in *The Truman Show*. Surveillance is provided by 'quasi' camera movements, when the protagonist's observing gaze switches from one window frame to the next. The use of binoculars and a telephoto lens also makes close viewing possible. This is particularly obvious in scenes where actions take place involving two (or more) window-screens, which resemble the monitors in a control room simultaneously viewing several different places.

In contrast to Bentham's panopticon, Jeffries's surveilling voyeurism does not actually exercise control over the objects of his gaze (the murder has happened). Innocent to the fact that they are under observation, the other tenants take no notice of the man seated at his rear window surveying the courtyard scene all day long. Although they might return his gaze, they do not seem to take notice of the man himself and his voyeuristic activities. Furthermore, his voyeuristic investigation is only safe as long as he can be sure that nobody catches him. Therefore, whenever he is in danger of being seen by the prime target of his investigation - Thorwald sometimes peers around the courtyard in order to ensure that he is not being watched - Jeffries turns off the lights in his flat and moves his wheelchair back into the shadow to remain invisible.

A conspiracy of voyeuristic investigation

Although both women in Jeffries's world initially assume that the murder story is merely a product of his boredom and imagination, the protagonist eventually mobilizes the help of his nurse and his girlfriend. Through Jeffries's persistent investigation Lisa and Stella are increasingly drawn into and fascinated by the story. As the women also take turns using the technical gadget to observe and investigate, they gradually turn into Jeffries's "co-investigative voyeurs".[94]

---

[93] This 'panoptic' reading has also been applied to the film by Denzin, *Cinematic Society*, 118-119; and Mladen Dolar, "A Father Who Is Not Quite Dead" (*Everything You Always Wanted to Know about Lacan*), 144. See also Foucault, 257-261. As Jeffries initially watches the tenants across the courtyard for the purpose of distraction, the voyeuristic situation in *Rear Window* also resembles the predecessor of Bentham's panopticon. In Louis Le Vau's ménagerie at Versailles the king watches different species of caged animals for his entertainment. Pallasmaa (referring to Foucault), 164. See also Foucault, 261

[94] Denzin even argues that their gaze does not merely supplement but displace Jeffries's gaze. Denzin, *Cinematic Society*, 124

By stepping into the visual sphere of the spectacle, they assist the investigation as mobile extensions or executive instruments of the immobilized voyeur-detective. While Jeffries remains the onlooker, Lisa and Stella take action across the courtyard. Delivering a note ("What have you done with her?"), digging in the garden and searching Thorwald's flat, they become the venturesome investigators of the protagonist's visual crime story. And it is the women, Lisa in particular, who finally bring the investigation to its close.

The women do not, however, merely enable the formerly passive Jeffries to make contact with the visual opposite, they also enrich the investigation by adding their considerations from a female point of view to his more rational logic of interpretation.[95] In their logic of interpretation the wife's wedding ring is needed as most obvious visual evidence of murder. "It is their feminine intuitions concerning Mrs Thorwald and her ring that lend authority to Jeff's interpretation of Thorwald's project. The female voyeur interprets what Jeff only sees."[96]

Visual paranoia turns into a real threat

With the women's interaction, safe observation from a distance - resembling cinema viewing - gradually turns into actual personal involvement. The visual experience of suspense that Jeffries has 'captured' through his rear window thus increasingly turns into a realistic danger, a threat to Lisa's and Jeffries's life.

When Lisa finds the wedding ring in Thorwald's flat, the salesman catches her red-handed. Now Jeffries is finally provided with the visual thrill he has been longing for, but seeing his girlfriend in the hands of the supposed murderer he feels threatened. But this is not the end: the sign she gives Jeffries before being taken into police custody - with her hands behind her back she shows him Mrs Thorwald's wedding ring on her finger - cannot be kept secret from the salesman's gaze. The discovery of the most important evidence thus causes the collapse of the voyeuristic-panoptic situation.

By tracing the direction of Lisa's gesture, the salesman knows that he is being observed from somewhere across the courtyard. When the overzealous Jeffries finally reveals his identity and location to Thorwald on the phone, the surveillance inherent in his voyeuristic gaze breaks down completely.[97]

---

[95] Lisa also concludes with what the spectator saw and suspects: that the woman in black must have been someone else - not Mrs Thorwald.

[96] Denzin, *Cinematic Society*, 124

[97] Resembling the audience in the cinema, which is seated at a safe distance to the thrilling events on the screen, it seems that Jeffries is so much caught up in his

The unmasking of the voyeur

Thorwald's returned gaze effects the exposure of the voyeur's visibility, and Jeffries literally finds himself a vulnerable victim trapped inside his 'flat-cell', helplessly awaiting the murderer's attempt to strike back. When Thorwald then enters the flat, the immobilized photographer simultaneously fights against visibility and tries to defend himself by releasing four flash lights to blind the approaching assailant.[98] It does not help him. The salesman's approach from the unfamiliar rear, behind Jeffries's door, is like the violent entry of the irrational and evil into Jeffries's world of distanced voyeurism and logical conclusions.[99] The former two-dimensional murderer has left the visual sphere of the spectacle and entered, as a real person, the sphere of the observer. When Thorwald throws poor Jeffries out of the rear window the voyeur is punished for his indiscrete gazing in a dual sense. Falling into the courtyard he enters the sphere of the spectacle he has been watching, thus becoming a part of it. As a result, the protagonist is also exposed to the neighbourhood community that returns his gaze and in turn become the onlookers of the spectacle visible through Jeffries's rear window.[100]

4. Scopophilic paranoia as visual investigation of reality

Scopophilic paranoia, visual investigation and the cinema

Similar to Antonioni's photographer who reconstructs the murder by arranging and interpreting the blow-ups into a photographic narrative in the blow-up sequence, Hitchcock's voyeur also follows cinematic principles in creating and watching a silent film using his logic of interpretation.

As I have already mentioned, Jeffries's voyeurism mirrors the cinematic situation. Resembling a spectator in the cinema who receives the images

voyeurism and its distance to the observed danger that he only slowly realizes the threat into which it has gradually turned.

[98] Miran Bozovic, "The Man Behind His Own Retina" (*Everything You Always Wanted to Know about Lacan*), 175

[99] Schmidt, Johann N., "Das Fenster zum Hof" in *Reclams Lexikon der Filmklassiker. Beschreibungen und Kommentare* Vol. 2 1947-1964, ed. Thomas Koebner. (Stuttgart: Reclam, 1995), 208

[100] Miran Bozovic, "The Man Behind His Own Retina" (*Everything You Always Wanted to Know about Lacan*), 175. Sharff mentions that the spectator's identification with Jeffries collapses completely when "the most crucial reverse shot in the film [... finally discloses ...] the geographically correct other side of the 'across', the fourth wall of the film". At the end of *Rear Window*, the protagonist is unmistakably rendered a member of the courtyard's 'rear community' and thus definitely a part of the film, the spectacle the spectator is watching. Sharff, 93 (see also 181-182)

presented to him on a screen, Jeffries is "confronted with the enigmatic signs in the building opposite his rear window".[101]

Jeffries is, however, not merely a passive onlooker. The protagonist's voyeuristic activity rather resembles the work of film making and editing.[102] As he tries to make sense of what he sees, his 'visual investigation' is, as it were, an act of creative seeing. By simultaneously observing and interpreting he constructs a criminal plot whose visual fragments resemble the sequences of a film.

The voyeur-investigator integrates the work of director, cameraman and cutter within his consciousness. Accordingly, his flat functions as both camera and projector or projection booth.[103] The direction and movement of Jeffries's gaze resembles camera work. In using the alternative optics of binoculars and a telephoto lens, Jeffries provides the film with different shot sizes (close-ups and medium shots) and selects the content of the image frames. Moreover, as his gaze wanders from one window to another it resembles the montage of a film, which connects sequences and determines the interpretation.[104]

Finally, as the film he creates is a silent film, Jeffries's and the women's comments, which interpret the visual information accordingly, function like off-screen voice-overs to the mute images.

"Tell me what you see and what you think it means" - Visual investigation

Jeffries's visual investigation and logic of interpretation follows a pattern of cumulative layering of visual information that gradually turns into 'visual knowledge'. This means that each newly observed detail is added to the visual memory of earlier visual perceptions. It implies that the protagonist's observations are always influenced by and interpreted on the basis of previously gained visual information (which, again, always comprises a visual perception and its interpretation - both based on visual memory of still earlier perceptions).

---

[101] Mladen Dolar, "A Father Who Is Not Quite Dead" (*Everything You Always Wanted to Know about Lacan*), 143

[102] The reversed symmetry in *Rear Window* also enables to read Jeff's flat as camera obscura in which the Thorwalds' relationship is reflected in reverse. See Miran Bozovic, "The Man Behind His Own Retina" (*Everything You Always Wanted to Know about Lacan*), 162; and Pallasmaa, 164

[103] Martine Lerude-Flechet, 107; and Pallasmaa, 164

[104] Pallasmaa, 154. In this respect, Paul Virilio points out that finally human consciousness functions like a film according to the principles of montage theory (or as Alexander Kluge would have it, there have always been films inside people's minds). See Sentürk, 46

This pattern not only resembles a puzzle or mosaic in which the fragments are arranged into a coherent context, the structure of the protagonist's visual investigation can also be referred to as a palimpsest.[105] Within Jeffries's logic of interpretation each perceived piece of visual information is determined by previous observations, and vice versa: further visual information from later perceptions influences that which has been observed before. This means that the meaning or interpretation of earlier perceptions retrospectively changes or becomes at all significant - similar to the murder explaining the salesman's strange nocturnal activity.

The assumed visual evidence of murder thus arises within Jeffries's logic of interpretation on the basis of his visual memory comprising earlier observations of his neighbourhood from which he had gained a certain visual knowledge about Thorwald and his wife.

The basic layer of this interpretive logic within which the murder develops is explained by Jeffries still innocent, yet voyeuristic observation that he knows the woman is bedridden and that her husband was caring for her. Moreover, the voyeur observed Thorwald trying to call someone on the phone behind his wife's back, her catching him red-handed and their following argument.[106] It is the visual information on which he bases his assumption that Thorwald might be having an affair.[107] And this is the basic hint that the salesman might wish to get rid of his moaning wife, whom he probably no longer wants to care for.

On the basis of this visual knowledge of the couple, the visual information to come is perceived and interpreted: the salesman's strange nocturnal movements with his samples case, followed by his ignoring his wife, the accompanying bustle with the saw and knife, his cleaning the samples case and the walls of his bathroom as well as the packing of the trunk. The most striking detail in this flow of visual information, however, is Mrs Thorwald's disappearance from the protagonist's visual field. It is the crucial element and obvious prerequisite for Jeffries's assumption of murder.

The same underlying principle applies to the incident with the little dog that is found dead in the garden. Jeffries's (and the women's) conclusion that the salesman must have murdered the animal (which again is interpreted as evidence that he is his wife's murderer) also arises from

---

[105] Writing on a palimpsest can be removed and overwritten. It appears, however, that previous writings leave traces on the palimpsest that can become visible again. The palimpsest therefore is a suitable metaphor for the simultaneous presence or layering of Jeffries's visual impressions throughout his investigative observations.

[106] Due to the heat, his window is permanently open and Jeffries occasionally catches snatches of conversation and hears them arguing.

[107] For the audience, this assumption is confirmed when they are provided with another clue - the woman in the black dress - that Jeffries misses.

retrospective interpretation of his previous observations. He had watched Thorwald gazing down at the dog in the garden that was digging in the flowerbed where Jeffries had seen the salesman pottering about the day before. On another occasion, the protagonist had also seen Thorwald pushing the animal away from the flowers.

Concerning the episode of the dog's death, Jeffries even comes up with photographic evidence in the form of two slides that show a similar view of the garden on different days around the night in question. As they seem to show dissimilarities in the flowerbed's appearance, the assumption that something might have been buried underneath the flowers seems reasonable. The fact that Thorwald hides in the dark of his flat - the faint glow of his cigarette indicates his presence - while all the neighbours come out to hear the dog owner's lamentations, puts him under suspicion of having killed the animal, which supposedly had to die because it sensed too much.

In the course of his visual investigation Jeffries not only surveys the salesman's actions. Similar to Antonioni's photographer studying the gaze and expression of the mysterious woman in the park on his blow-ups, Jeffries also scrutinizes the suspect's behaviour and seeks a clue. Trying to read his facial expression, he keenly observes Thorwald's reaction to the delivered note. Influenced by his visual knowledge of the probable murderer, Jeffries sees in Thorwald's looking around the courtyard the gaze of someone afraid of being watched. Accordingly, the salesman's attempts to remain invisible by hiding in the dark of his flat are perceived/interpreted as indicative of a man who is or feels guilty.[108]

Thus, in his logic of interpretation the accumulation of various layers of visual information enables Jeffries to trace and detect the crime. In his logic, the lack of visual information - the murder itself (and the woman in the black dress) - is perfected by his imagination.[109]

---

[108] The faint glow of a cigarette in the dark window frame of Thorwald's flat, which appears several times throughout the film, has been interpreted by several investigators of the film as a sign of the salesmen's reciprocation of Jeffries's gaze. See Denzin, *Cinematic Society*, 125; and Miran Bozovic, "The Man Behind His Own Retina" (*Everything You Always Wanted to Know about Lacan*), 168-169

[109] The newlyweds with their mostly 'blank screen closed blinds' function as an example of how a lack of visual information is completed by imaginary action. Although they are more often not to be seen, it seems to be clear what happens inside their flat. Meaning is derived from the few pieces of available visual information, and the gaps are filled in by interpretation. See Sharff, 34

Murder mystery disclosed - Order re-established?

In *Rear Window* the mystery is disclosed. At the end of the film the crime is detected and the villain is in the hands of the police. As Jeffries's suspicion turns out to be rational and objectively true, the peeping tom is finally redeemed. With his immoral behaviour 'punished' by another broken leg, "the final effects of Jeffries's voyeurism are almost entirely admirable.[110] If he hadn't spied on his neighbours, a murderer would have gone free."[111] Thus, in the end the protagonist appears to be a hero who almost risked his life to serve the community by detecting a hideous crime and revealing the murderer.

In this respect, paranoia in *Rear Window* reflects the 1950s "political climate of mutual distrust [which] produced a culture of fear suspecting its own members".[112] This reading of Hitchcock's film classifies it as representative of the early period of paranoia in film.

As the film thematizes visuality and the ambiguity of appearances, however, *Rear Window* anticipates the postmodern epistemological crisis of a society of the spectacle. Denzin describes the film as a herald of the "hyperreal, mass-mediated world [...] where the images would replace lived experience, and understandings would be produced by those who controlled the [visual] information technologies of a culture".[113] As Denzin mentions, with reference to Baudrillard, *Rear Window* thus "enunciates a postmodern epistemology where things are real if they appear to be real".[114]

In this respect, Jeffries is an anticipation of the postmodern voyeur, whose visual paranoia gives expression to a latent general suspicion of the appearance of things.[115] In a world of visuality that is filled with deception,

---

[110] With two broken legs, Jeffries's 'attempt' to break out of his 'eye' and leave the sphere of the spectator is rendered a failure. He is doomed to be an immobilized onlooker for a long time.

[111] Wood, 62

[112] F. Colier refers to the American anxiety of society being infiltrated by communist spies. In this context Jeffries resembles the civilian who feels responsible and is doing his duty in protecting society from enemy contamination (with evil personified by the murderer). F. Colier, *These Memories Can Wait*, http://www.altered-ego.net/ART%20Films/memento.htm (18 July 2010)

[113] Denzin, *Cinematic Society*, 128

[114] Denzin, *Cinematic Society*, 119

[115] Denzin identifies the voyeur as "the iconic, postmodern self" [Denzin, *Cinematic Society*, 2] and as a "seeker of truth" who "in a society where the truth too often masquerades as a fiction" [...] "sees what others cannot or will not see". Denzin, *Images of Postmodern Society*, 155-156

he tries to 'escape from the prison of seeing'.[116] With an inspective gaze he scrutinizes the surface of things and discovers an evil man, behind the facade of a devoted husband, who murders his bedridden wife.

Jeffries's visual investigation is like an excavation of layers of reality. In tracing the hidden truth he discovers the ambiguous character of the visual world, in which the boundaries between good and evil are blurred. As he is forced to commit an offence himself in order to detect the secret crime, he learns that it depends on one's point of view as to what is perceived and how it is interpreted.

Thus, at the end of the film a sense of latent doubt remains about the 'superficial impression' of its happy ending. Despite the case being solved and order re-established in the world of the courtyard there is a humorous hint of reality's continually ambiguous nature: Lisa pretends to be reading a non-fiction work on the Himalayas in order to make Jeffries believe that the superficial fashion girl has turned into a tough girl preparing herself for adventures to come. As soon as she notices that he has fallen asleep, however, she starts browsing through a fashion magazine she has been hiding from his gaze. It is a last symbolic remark about the potential deception inherent in visuality.[117]

A further aspect of both readings of the film is that *Rear Window* anticipates a society in which the private sphere becomes increasingly public, and which controls itself by means of panoptic surveillance systems. While in Hitchcock's film the lifting of the veil of privacy through the voyeur's investigative gaze still has a positive connotation, since it uncovers a hideous crime, in later films this attempt to gain an overview and control will turn into a cause of the scopophobic paranoia of *The Truman Show*.

---

[116] Leo Braudy referring to a statement by Hitchcock in Leo Braudy, *The World in a Frame: What We See in Films* (Chicago and London: Chicago University Press, 2002), 81

[117] Another aspect to be mentioned here is the 'revelation' of "Miss Torso's" husband. His arrival is another unexpected discovery, as the woman appeared to be like someone who cannot be satisfied with just one lover (who in return does not seem to be too interested in her). See also Sharff, 98-101

5. The scopophilic paranoia plot in *Rear Window*

Jeff, temporarily disabled, passes his time looking out of the window. Watching his neighbours from the block is his favourite entertainment while being confined to a wheel chair. While doing so he collects important data for his upcoming activity as visual investigator.

Jeff's view from his backyard window: the scene of upcoming events

He often observes the couple across the yard – a salesman and his wife, who is confined to bed.

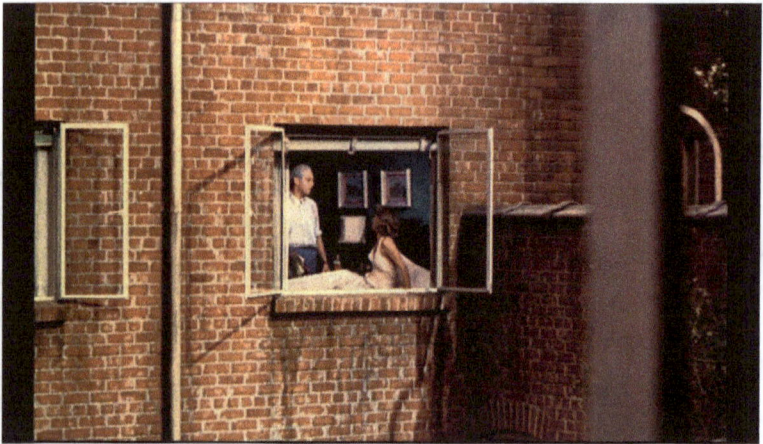

The husband seems to care for his wife as well as possible, alongside his job.
However, Jeff also witnesses their regular arguments.

All the time Jeff has been watching the backyard scene the woman has never left her home and is always lying or sitting on her bed...

One evening Jeff observes this scene: the sick woman overhears her husband talking on the phone in the living-room next door to her bedroom. She interrupts him and makes a scene. It seems that they are having a serious marital quarrel.

After these signs of discord, Jeff – still lying awake late at night – observes the salesman who, despite driving rain, leaves the flat with his samples case...

... only to return home some time later.

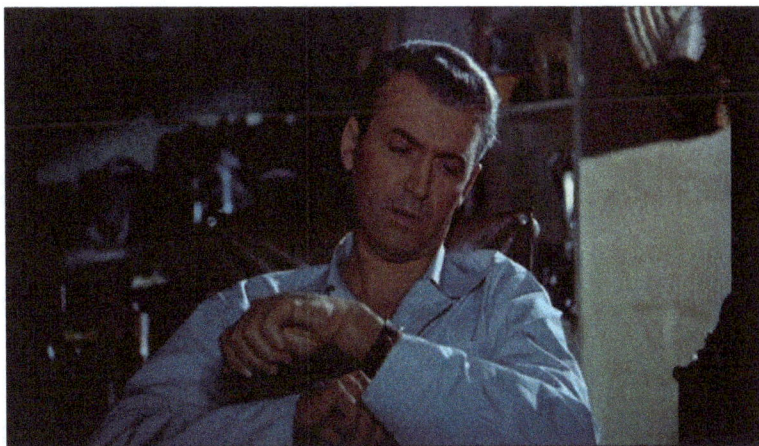

As this happens again, Jeff - partly by way of a change from the boredom he suffers from and partly out of suspicion - carefully notes the salesman's night-time movements. He looks at the clock every time the man leaves, and also when he returns home.

The next morning, the sick woman's window (on the right) stays shuttered. The salesman looks around the backyard in a manner that seems strange to Jeff. He suspects – as he reports to Stella – that the man must have done something to his wife.

As his observations become more serious and purposeful Jeff does not want to be noticed as an onlooker. He wants the suspicious person to feel unobserved and behave normally.

The next clue: Jeff sees the salesman cleaning his samples case. What did he carry inside it that requires it to be cleaned like that?

Jeff uses his binoculars to get a better view of the details. From now on he is 'on duty'.

The man puts watches and jewellery back into the suitcase. He must have been carrying something else in the suitcase last night.

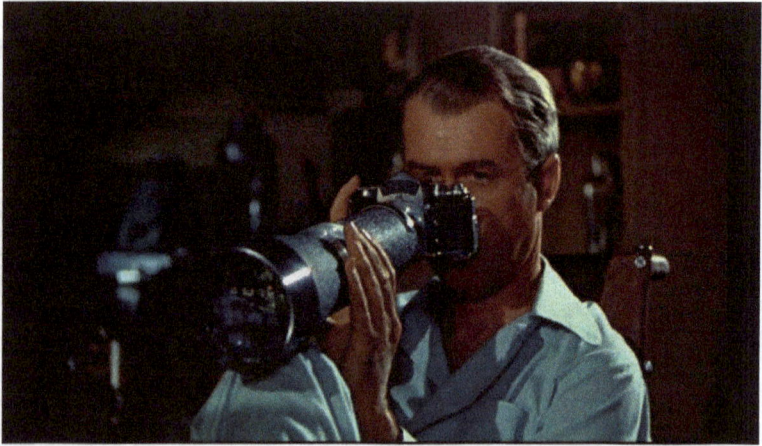

In order to see even more, and to probe deeper into the occurrences across the yard, Jeff swaps the binoculars for a telephoto lens.

What he views through the lens confirms his worst assumptions: he watches the man across the yard cleaning a saw...

... and a big knife and wrapping them up in newspapers.

The evening after the night of strange events the blinds of the woman's room are still down. No signs of life from her.

The next clue: In the evening, the salesman brings a rope and uses it to pack and stabilize a big wardrobe trunk. He has also rolled up the mattress from his wife's bed.

When this happens, even Lisa cannot help but believe that something strange must be going on.

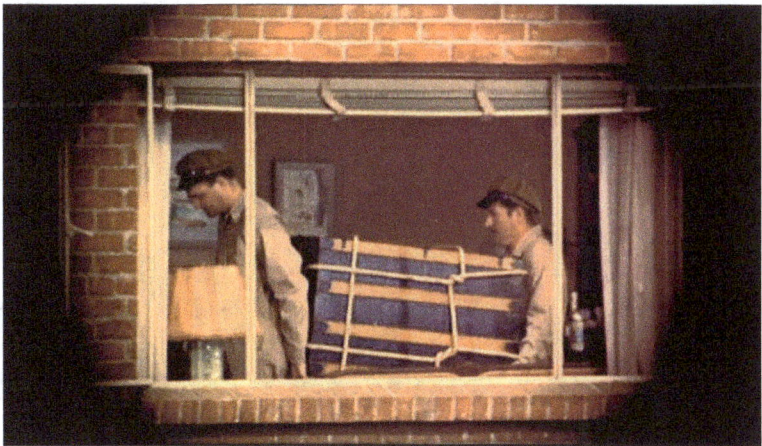

When Jeff observes the transport of the wardrobe trunk from the salesman's flat...

...Stella gets active, compensating for Jeff's immobility. She runs into the street to find out the name of the transport company. Unfortunately she is not quick enough.

Doyle, whom Jeff asks to take over the case, does not believe in a criminal explanation of the neighbourhood events. Although he assumes that it is merely Jeff's exuberant fantasy trying to fight boredom, Doyle promises to ask around and keep his ears open...

... to come back with the news that the salesman's name is Lars Thorwald, that his wife has gone on holiday, that her husband had taken her to the train early in the morning, that the wardrobe trunk held her clothes and other belongings and that he even fished out a postcard from Thorwald's post box, which his wife had obviously sent him on arrival at her destination, telling him that she was fine. Nonetheless, Jeff does not stop his investigation. Since he does not believe that this is the plain truth, he continues observing Thorwald.

He watches the little dog of another neighbour that is digging in the flowerbed Thorwald used to care for. - What does the dog scent?

(Thorwald had seen the dog digging into the soil on another occasion and had shoved him away.)

For some reason, Jeff remembers having taken pictures of the backyard a couple of days earlier. With the help of this visual resource - comparing the colour negative (above) to the actual status (below) - he finds that something might have been buried under the flowers where the dog has been burrowing.

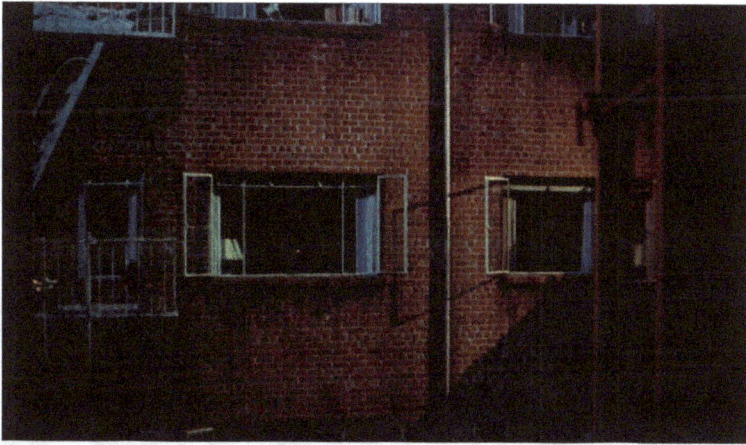

In the evening, the suspect sits smoking in the dark of his flat. Even when there is uproar in the backyard when the little dog is found dead, the window stays dark with only a glimpse of the cigarette. Why is Thorwald so unaffected by the animal's fate and the sorrow of its owner?

He watches Thorwald speaking on the phone and taking his wife's jewellery out of her handbag, among other pieces also her wedding ring. Lisa will later draw the conclusion that there is something very odd going on when a woman leaves her handbag and – even worse and less credible – her wedding ring behind. That is not normal.

More strange goings-on: Why does Thorwald clean the walls of his bathroom late at night? Does he need to remove stains and traces of blood?

When, later in the evening, Thorwald busily packs a suitcase, the three investigators feel the need to act and intervene.

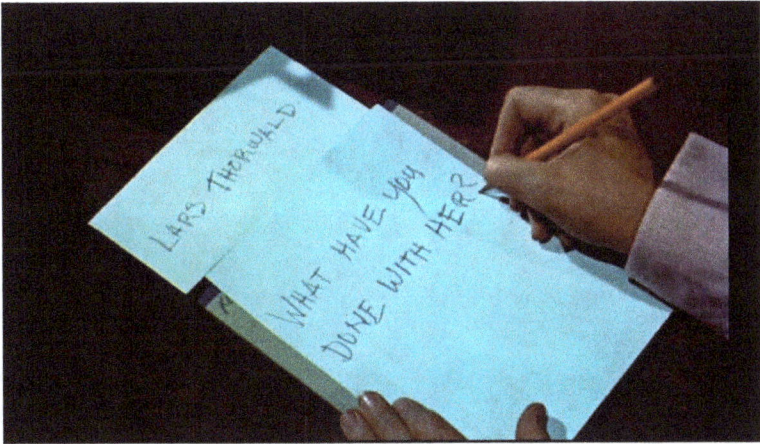

Jeff writes a short note to provoke the suspect and to draw him out of his flat... and gain time...

Lisa quickly delivers the message to its intended recipient.

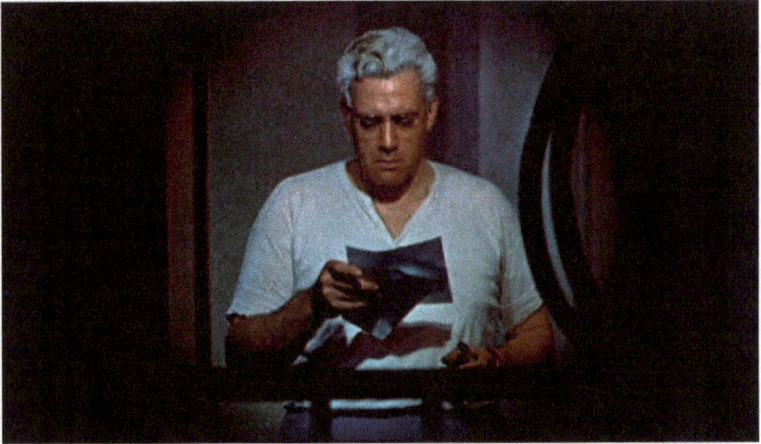

Thorwald is being observed while reading, and soon after Jeff gives him a call to get him to go under a pretext to a meeting point.

When Thorwald has left, the women start digging in the backyard to find out what the dog had smelled and tried to dig out from under the flowers.
Since they do not find anything, Lisa spontaneously decides to climb into the flat in Thorwald's absence, and to sneak into his rooms and snoop around.

Jeff watches her as she finds the handbag that used to hang beside the sick woman's bed. Lisa indicates to him that it is empty.

Unfortunately, Lisa is caught off guard by Thorwald returning home from the supposed meeting (Jeff wanted to warn her, but got temporarily side-tracked by goings-on in the lonely heart's flat).

At the point of culmination, observation is intensified: two pairs of eyes, supported by binoculars and a telephoto lens watching the danger zone.

Despite her risky situation, Lisa sends a secret visual message across the yard. She has found the wedding ring.

Unluckily, Thorwald notices the sign, which leads him to her accomplice...

It does not take long before Jeff has an unwanted visitor. The attack on Jeff and the subsequent investigations by the police finally verify Jeff's suspicion: it turns out that Thorwald had murdered his wife, and that he had temporarily buried part of her body under the flowers.

III. Photographic Paranoia in Blow-Up

1. Unexhausted Circulation of distraction and interpretation

> "What Antonioni shows us is that reality must
> be interpreted, that what seems to be obvious
> is not necessarily so."
>
> Peter Brunette, *The Films of Michelangelo Antonioni*, 174

Michelangelo Antonioni's *Blow-Up* (1966), which is based on the short story *Las babas del diablo* by Julio Cortàzar, has been described as "a series of photographs about a series of photographs".[118] Like *Rear Window*, *Blow-Up* is an extraordinarily visual film.[119] Composed of many long duration shots, which are often enacted by a static camera, a geometric conception of the field of vision leaves space for a free floating gaze.[120]

As in Hitchcock's film, *Blow-Up* revolves around a crime or, rather, its detection. Through the scene in the park, the viewer is subtly introduced to the film's genre. Almost imperceptibly a crime story creeps into the plot. It is not until the blow-up scene, however, that the film turns to murder. As in *Rear Window*, the crime only comes into being through investigation.

Belonging to David Boyd's category of the cinema of interpretation, *Blow-Up* inverts the usual relationship between the two narrative lines of the detective story. The story of the crime is reduced "to little more than the occasion for the story of investigation".[121] As the photographer's detection of the crime is not concerned with the usual questions of 'how, who and why', "what happened in the park is of less urgent concern than what happens in the dark room".[122]

---

[118] John Freccero as quoted in David Boyd, "Images of Interpretation: *Blow-Up*" in *Film and the Interpretive Process. A Study of 'Blow-Up', 'Rashomon', 'Citizen Kane', '81/2', 'Vertigo' and 'Persona'* (New York, Bern, Frankfurt am Main, Paris: Peter Lang, 1989), 24

[119] In fact, all of Antonioni's films are extraordinarily visual in comparison to other films. The specific characteristic of *Blow-Up* lies in the film's focus on the visual within the narrative. In the blow-up scene, which is almost mute, the concentration on visuality is most striking.

[120] Fabian Stoermer, "Unschuldige Beweise. Michelangelo Antonioni, *Blow up*, Peter Greenaway, *Der Kontrakt des Zeichners*" in *Nach dem Film* No 8: *Fotokino* (1/12/2005); http://www.nachdemfilm.de/content/unschuldige-beweise (14 August 2010)

[121] Boyd, 20

[122] Boyd, 10

Narrative structure

Blow-Up has a multi-layered narrative structure, which is simultaneously characterized by both complexity and openness. As the boundaries between reality and imagination become blurred, what happens in the park, the protagonist's perceptions and interpretations, his photographic material and the narrative he creates from it are equally important and become closely interconnected. The film is composed of an intricate and interpretive chain of association, in which experience, representation and interpretation merge into one another.[123]

Peter Brunette describes the film as constituting a 'dialectic of binary oppositions'.[124] This pattern is introduced in the exposition with the mimes intercut by Thomas leaving the doss house and the mimes running into the nuns and the Queen's Guard. The protagonist connects the two opposing spheres: he has put on a disguise to spend the night among the homeless, and when he jumps into his Rolls Royce to return to his studio he 'runs into' the mimes.[125] This structure is taken up again at the end of the film when Thomas meets the mimes again and joins in their imaginary tennis match (thus, once again participating in another reality).

Moreover, the protagonist's photographic images of the park scene and the reality they represent stand in opposition to the film by the use of contrast in the cinematic representation of the respective narrative sequences. The almost silent blow-up scene, with its focus on the visual and the black and white stills of the scene in the park, opposes the colourful, audible and lively reality of London life.

The effect of this dichotomy established at the beginning of the film is to induce a sense of an ambiguous reality on the part of the viewer. This ambiguity is also reflected in the opening titles, which seem to be cut out of the grass, opening the view onto another reality. The semitransparent and reflexive surfaces all over the photographer's studio also evoke the ambiguity of visual appearances.

Blow-Up, is also characterized by a pattern of distraction. Although the narration follows the chronology of events of approximately 24 hours in the

---

[123] Taylor identifies this as a typical feature of the paranoia film. Taylor, 48

[124] Peter Brunette, "Blow-Up (1966)" in The Films of Michelangelo Antonioni (New York: Cambridge University Press, 1998), 110

[125] See also Gunther Salje: Antonioni. Regieanalyse, Regiepraxis (Bassum: Verlag Media-Institut, 1996), 213. While the mimes symbolize joyful fantasy and imagination (the sphere of art) the old and poor men leaving the doss house represent the hardship of real life ('bare' reality). Accordingly, the nuns and the Queen's Guard can be read as symbols for contrasting 'worlds'. Thus, the pattern of binary opposition alludes to the co-existence of alternative realities.

life of the photographer, thus evoking an illusion of continuity, it is not a common plot-driven narrative. Composed of seemingly incoherent sequences (erotic episode with teenage girls, rock concert, marihuana party etc.), the camera often focusing on seemingly 'irrelevant' objects (such as the gays walking their dogs, part of a guitar, the coin trick or the mysterious neon letters near the park) the structure of the film rather resembles a chain of associations. In this respect, the form reflects the diegetic content of the narrative. In accordance with his erratic way of life, the protagonist's quest is persistently disturbed.[126] As Thomas is constantly absorbed in one new idea or another, he is continually distracted from what he is actually doing. Most of his actions are not finished before he starts something else; he interrupts the photo-shooting, for example, to drive to an antique shop. His visit to the shop is 'interrupted' by the park scene. In the cafe he does not eat the food he has ordered because he follows the guy who seems to have chased him. The woman's visit (and their attempt to have sex) is interrupted by the delivery of the propeller. Even the study of his photographic material, the blow-up scene, is interrupted by the girls' visit and the following sexual interlude (in the middle of his telephone call with Ron to tell him about his discovery of the man with the pistol). His search for the woman he sees among the crowd of people in the street is interrupted by a scuffle over a guitar at a rock-concert. And finally, the marihuana party distracts him from convincing his friend and returning to the park to take a photograph of the corpse.[127]

Eventually, the narrative of the film follows a repetitive circular structure. The protagonist returns to the antique shop, his studio and the park; he meets the mysterious woman and his friend Ron twice. Furthermore, the interpretation of the park scene is repeated at least three times: the assumption of a love-scene turns into a supposed prevention of a crime, which again turns into the realization that the photographer must have witnessed a murder.

Finally, *Blow-Up* makes a circular movement on both the diegetic and meta-diegetic level. When the erratic narrative focuses around the blow-up sequence, thus gaining significance, this meaning is almost erased towards

---

[126] Maybe the most prominent example of this pattern of distraction is the propeller that Thomas buys in the antique shop, which seems to be of importance neither to him later on nor to the story itself. A further aspect of this pattern is that it reflects the fact that in connection with visual paranoia every detail might be significant. As paranoia perceives the world as a system of signs to be read, everything is potentially important.

[127] The reflection of the protagonist's distraction throughout the film's narrative structure accordingly distracts the recipient from following the film's central thread - his perception of the film thus approximates the protagonist's perception of the world around him.

the end of the film when the 'reality of the murder' is again called into question.

The mystery of a crime - A plot within a plot

Since the story of interpretive investigation centres around the snapshots of the park, the blow-up scene constitutes the nucleus around which the film's various layers 'unexhaustedly circulate'.[128] This sequence thus functions as the key element in the narrative's complex structure. Focusing on the photographic material as the protagonist tries to figure out its meaning, the erratic narrative changes its mode.[129] The narration slows down and 'stays' with the photographer in his studio while he produces the blow-ups very passionately and meticulously, running to and fro between the dark room and the white walls of his studio.[130]

Through the blow-up scene it also becomes clear that *Blow-Up* makes use of the 'framing device'. As the protagonist arranges and interprets his photographs, the 'plot' within the narrative becomes a narrative plot.[131] Similar to Jeffries's investigative and interpretive observation in *Rear Window*, the photographic narrative resembles a 'film within a film' and, accordingly, the photographer's actions the work of a film maker.

Narrative perspective

Like *Rear Window*, *Blow-Up* is a self-reflexive film that engages its audience in reflection on visual perception and cinematic reception. It draws the spectator into the protagonist's visual investigation. In the blow-up scene, in particular, the subjective camera (which shows shots attributed to the protagonist's point-of-view) merges the audience's perspective into that of the photographer.[132]

---

[128] Lorenzo Cuccu as quoted in Brunette, 125

[129] Despite the omitted parts of processing in the dark room it almost seems as if acting time and reading time are more or less congruent in the blow-up scene.

[130] Gerard Oppermann describes the film's clear division between the dark room where the prints and blow-ups are produced and the studio as the sphere of interpretation - another set of binary oppositions. Gerard Oppermann, "Die Mittelszene des Filmes *Blow-Up*" in *Michelangelo Antonioni*, eds. Jan Berg and Hans-Otto Hügel (Hildesheim: Universität Hildesheim, Institut für Theater und Medienwissenschaft, 1995), 9

[131] Robert T. Eberwein, "The Master Text of *Blow-Up*" in *Close Viewings*, ed. Peter Lehman (Tallahassee: Florida State University Press, 1990), 271

[132] This device is sustained at the audio level when a seemingly subjective aural perception evokes the protagonist's memory of the rustling park trees in the studio during the blow-up scene, or when the sound of the invisible ball at the end of the film indicates Thomas's imaginary participation in the mimes' tennis match.

The audience, however, does not merely share the photographer's 'visual knowledge' at this point. As the narrative of the film alternates between first and third person, the viewer also observes the photographer from an outside perspective, viewed by an 'autonomous camera'.[133] Thus, 'being more removed' than Hitchcock's protagonist, the spectator's superior position includes in his visual field Antonioni's photographer as an object of the cinematic gaze. The recipient is thus made to be a voyeur in a dual sense. He adopts a split perspective which is most prominent in as well as most important for the film's central scene. It is created by the perception of the photographic material through Thomas's consciousness on the one hand, and watching the voyeur as he goes about his investigation, scrutinizing the blow-ups as well as pondering and interpreting on the other. It enables the viewer to simultaneously participate and observe the interpretive investigation.

As the diegetic content of Blow-Up works parallel to the meta-diegetic level of the film, the circle around the 'epistemological theme' not only concerns the plot of the narrative with the protagonist getting lost in a cycle of interpretation. Just as the photographer tries to come to terms with the mystery of his photographic representations in the blow-up scene, the spectator searches for meaning in the film. In this respect, concerning the blow-up scene, Antonioni's photographer functions as a stand-in for the spectator - similar to the ambiguous voyeuristic-cinematic situation in Rear Window. Thus, Blow-Up, too, intends to make the spectator sense "a self-conscious awareness of his own interpretive activity".[134]

2. Capturing reality

The photographer as voyeur

The protagonist of Blow-Up is, like Jeffries in Rear Window, a photographer. Focusing on the visual, he perceives the world through his camera's gaze. Restless and continually on the move, Thomas is constantly looking for interesting objects or situations he could capture on film. His "aesthetic detachment makes him the pure spectator".[135]

The photographer's secret observation of the men in the doss house and his sexualized male gaze on his models exposes him as a voyeur. He wishes to intrude neither into the private life of his friends Bill and Patricia nor into the surreptitious atmosphere of the intimate situation between the young

---

[133] Gerard Oppermann adopts this term, which was applied to Antonioni's style by Ned Rifkin, in his text "Die Mittelszene des Filmes Blow-Up" (Michelangelo Antonioni), 10

[134] Boyd, 5

[135] Denzin, Cinematic Society, 135

woman and the elder man in the park, which he documents without authorization.[136]

The protagonist is, however, not merely a passive onlooker. Working as fashion photographer he is a creator of aesthetic images. He manipulates reality or, rather, creates or directs artificial realities in which his models act like puppets.[137] His life is thus focused on a world of simulacra, his photographic pictures are representations of a world that does not really exist. They are empty signs, simulating a false reality.

Jaded by his highly-polished life and bored by the routine of his job, Thomas has started working on a documentary portrait of London. Challenged by the task of fathoming reality, he leaves his studio and the fashion world of false appearances. As a countermove, he changes his appearance, thus adopting a false -identity in order to remain unnoticed. This enables him to capture authentic representations of reality, namely the social misery in a refuge for the homeless.

The scene in the park

The morning after his night in the doss house Thomas goes to the public park near the antique shop he has just visited. He discovers two strangers, a young woman and an elderly man, who seem to be teasing each other. Although he secretly observes them from a distance at first, he then gradually creeps up closer and enthusiastically records the intimate situation between the couple from all possible angles with his still camera.[138] What appears to be a peaceful love scene inspires him with the idea that he might use the images as a closing chapter in his book on London life.

Despite his attempt to remain 'invisible', the woman finally notices him. She rushes over to him and urgently appeals to him to give her the film roll.[139] Thomas tries to calm her down, but insists that he needs the

---

[136] Both actions - the attempt to remain 'invisible' to the objects of his camera's gaze (in the doss house and the park) and his sexualized male gaze on his friends' love scene and the models he 'seduces' with his camera - resemble the two aspects of the voyeuristic gaze.

[137] He even tells the woman from the park, whom he finds both attractive and photogenic, how to smoke the joint "against the beat".

[138] Although Thomas spies on the couple in the public sphere, his initially invisible gaze is of a voyeuristic nature, since he witnesses an intimate situation between two strangers who do not know they are being observed. Moreover, as the photographer takes unauthorized pictures his inquisitive gaze continues in the blow-up scene when he scrutinizes the enlargements.

[139] Thus, like Jeffries in *Rear Window*, Thomas gets drawn into in the spectacle he has observed (though right from the beginning).

photographs. When the woman suddenly discovers that her lover has disappeared, she runs off like a frightened deer to follow him.

The factor of suspicion

Having met the publisher, whom he has shown the pictures from the doss house and told about the snapshots he has just taken of the flirting couple, the protagonist returns to his studio. There he finds the woman from the park waiting for him. She has come to get the film roll. Contrary to the other women who offer Thomas sex in order to be photographed by him, she offers herself in order to get hold of the images he took of her without permission.[140] Just as they are about to 'start something', however, they are interrupted by the delivery of the propeller.

The more the woman tries to prevent him from looking at the images, the less the photographer wants let go of them. Apart from the fact that he does not want to abandon his plans for his book, he is increasingly fascinated by the mysterious woman. Her persistency in demanding the film arouses Thomas's interest. Why does she want to hold back what might be captured on the film roll? The challenge of solving the mystery behind her 'suspicious' behaviour - How did she know his address? Did she follow him secretly? - leads him to pretend to give in by handing her over a false film.

3. Photographic investigation: the Blow-Up

After the woman's departure the photographer immediately starts his investigation. He develops the negatives and produces the first blow-ups. Curious to see again what happened in the park, Thomas is not yet sure what exactly he is looking for. His former intention of finishing his book on London, however, is influenced by his desire to find out why the woman wanted the film roll. He hopes to find a clue explaining the woman's urgent interest in the images.[141]

Taking a close look at the first images pinned to his studio walls, the protagonist does not at first notice anything conspicuous. It seems that the photographs represent the fragments of the scene he observed in the park in the morning.

---

[140] Stoermer, http://www.nachdemfilm.de/content/unschuldige-beweise

[141] As Stoermer points out the images have already altered their significance before enlargement. They have changed from the expected peaceful scene into a fascinating picture puzzle. Stoermer, http://www.nachdemfilm.de/content/unschuldige-beweise

Distortion of reality by representation

Thomas's visual investigation initially leads to his being lost in the dilemma of the photographic image. This dilemma is rooted in the photographer's "assumption that the apparatus in fact registers what he sees and designates as meaning"; that is, what he thought he saw and captured on film is real.[142] Unlike his studio work for fashion magazines, he was not able to manipulate the spectacle in front of his lens but merely recorded things as they happened. The photographer thus believes that the snapshots from the park are authentic documentary material of a secretly witnessed love scene that he saw with his own eyes, albeit through the lens of the camera.

Photography, as Susan Sontag points out, is, however, a subjugation of reality.[143] It is therefore almost impossible to regard photographic images as 'objective' observation. Though Thomas witnesses the situation between the two strangers accidentally,[144] while he is aimlessly wandering about the park, he is not without prejudice. As always, he is not unprepared, has his camera with him, ready to capture whatever interesting object or scenario he might encounter. When he observes the couple, he is fascinated by the scene because something is happening that appears to be worth recording without his encouragement. He is "caught up in an idealist view of the medium, when, that is, he thinks he can select aspects of his visual environment and make them represent what he wants them to".[145] With his thoughts circling around his book, his perception of the scene is coloured by his perception of what he wants to see: the love-scene that might serve him as a peaceful closure.[146] When he releases the button, in his mind the scene

---

[142] Robert T. Eberwein, "The Master Text of *Blow-Up*" (*Close Viewings*), 268

[143] As Susan Sontag points out, photography can be regarded "as an exercise in power and control". She sees a connection between the professionalized look and cruelty. Concerning his disrespectful behaviour towards the 'puppet-like models' during a photo shooting, it must be agreed that Thomas is indeed "forcing his subjects to bend to his will" (Boyd referring to Sontag's *On Photography* (1977), 28). Sontag has also described the photographic image as the death mask of the object represented on it (this aspect has a dual meaning with regard to the picture of the corpse); see McQuire, 28. This understanding of the camera as a 'weapon' corresponds to Eberwein's description of Thomas's camera as his instrument to 'master reality'. See Robert T. Eberwein, "The Master Text of *Blow-Up*" (*Close Viewings*), 278

[144] It might be argued, however, that Thomas has followed them on purpose, having earlier seen them climbing up the slope. He could not have imagined or expected, however, that he would actually see them both further up the hill, and that they would offer him such an unexpected motif.

[145] Eberwein mentions this as one aspect of his work with his models, such as when he instructs them to smile. Robert T. Eberwein, "The Master Text of *Blow-Up*" (*Close Viewings*), 268

[146] Denzin, *Cinematic Society* (referring to Ned Rifkin, *Antonioni's Visual Language* (1982), 106), 135

makes an excellent contrast to the harsh reality of London life portrayed in his book. The freedom and harmony of the lovers in the park is meant to console and give a hopeful perspective after all.

The images of reality created by the camera become distorted by the subjectivity of the photographer's voyeuristic gaze. The photographs show what the photographer saw when he looked through the lens at a particular moment in time. The limitedness of the image frame deprives the fragment of the reality of its context. There might be significant details outside the frame. The single image is therefore unreliable in its meaning. Thus, despite its seemingly documentary character photographic representation is already an interpretation of the recorded event, since the act of taking a picture is an 'interpretation while observing'.[147] The protagonist is therefore unable to discover the crime hidden in the details on the images, as his attention is focused on the expected love scene.

Photographic panopticism

Thomas's voyeurism in the park turns him into the unwitting witness of a murder. Although he was present when the scene took place, and captured it with his camera, he is not an eye-witness. When he released the button he did not see what he finds his camera has recorded. The protagonist has to undergo a process of photographic investigation to discover in the details the hidden clues that disclose the secret murder scene.[148]

As the images do not represent what the photographer thought he recorded - that is, what he thought he saw and intended to 'photo-graph' - photography substitutes and sustains the protagonist's gaze. Using the protagonist's subjective perspective and the restrictions imposed by the frame, the camera, as mechanical apparatus, enacts a seemingly 'objective' gaze and records whatever gets into its field of vision. In this respect, the photographic pictures, as visual evidence, might be read as still images of a 'panoptic' surveillance camera in the presence of which visuality, according to Foucault, turns out to be a "trap" for the people involved in the events in the park.[149]

Functioning as photographic memory, his images enable Thomas to revisit and revise the scene in the park. Since the murder is hidden in the details, the limited range of a photographic fixation turns out to be an advantage for the protagonist. As the duration of the photographic representation

---

[147] This aspect of the medium is also inherent in its name photo-graphy - which is ultimately a form of 'writing' and, thus, a creative process. See also McQuire, 29

[148] Similar to Jeffries in *Rear Window*, who does not witness the 'deed' of the crime, Thomas captured the moments that preceded and followed the murder.

[149] See also Stoermer, http://www.nachdemfilm.de/content/unschuldige-beweise

overcomes the transience of the moment, it opens up the opportunity to scan retrospectively the entire field of vision on the image. Allowing only a limited view within the frame, the photographic image sharpens visual perception and raises consciousness and attention to details.

Finally, the protagonist makes up for the fragmentary character of his record of reality in the still images by means of enlargement (which also resembles a zoom by the surveillance camera) and interpretation, both of which culminate in the photographic narrative.

Tracing the mystery in the traces of light

Since the protagonist does not gain insight from his first superficial examination, he continues his investigation by looking at his photographs in a way he has probably never done before. He becomes immersed in the images and actually inspects them until he finds 'something to hang unto' (like his friend Bill, who retrospectively detects a meaning in his abstract paintings).[150]

Like a detective, Thomas concentrates on details and finally finds a clue in the woman's gaze in a close-up shot. While embracing the older man, she is looking over her shoulder and out of the frame of the picture. There is a strange expression on her face, which makes the photographer suspicious. He therefore searches for the object of the woman's gaze by following the direction of her eyes into another blow-up.

After scrutinizing the image with a magnifying glass he marks a space on the image in the bushes behind the fence. He produces a further blow-up but cannot yet make sense of it. There seems to be something odd about the situation, but Thomas is not yet able to solve its mystery. He therefore tries to call the woman from the park in order to ask her about the case. He discovers, however, that she has given him a false number - in return for the fake film roll he gave her.[151] This arouses the photographer's suspicion even more, and he continues to scrutinize the images. When he finally discovers a bright space on the detail of the fence he produces another still larger blow-up of the same image. On the latter he discovers the face of a man and a revolver visible between the bushes.

Seeking to re-interpret the increased visual information, he draws the provisional conclusion that he must have saved someone's life. Including

---

[150] Bill (as quoted from the film) explains Thomas how his works after a while suddenly make sense to him and that the interpretation of his art "is like finding a clue in a detective story".

[151] The woman will appear to him again in a crowd like an 'apparition' as he passes by in his car. When he follows her to ask about the events in the park, however, she disappears into the crowd in the street.

himself as part of the spectacle, Thomas sees himself as the hero in a would-be crime story, whose photographic shot prevented the shot from the pistol (as he tells his friend Ron on the phone).

On the one hand, these findings irritate Thomas, since he finds himself 'deceived'. It seems that reality outside his studio is not necessarily what it appears to be.[152] Recording the attempted murder, the photographic material no longer fits into his plan for the book. On the other hand, he is fascinated by the spectacle he has unconsciously witnessed with his camera. Spurred on by his "fabulous" results he continues his visual investigation. Seeking to figure out how the scene took place, and how it continued, he produces more blow-ups and searches for further clues.

From enlargement to decomposition

Like Jeffries in *Rear Window*, Thomas wants to see more than is visible in the photographic images. He attempts to get deeper into the visual investigation by producing more and even larger enlargements of the blow-ups, concentrating on certain details that seem to provide him with clues. His method resembles the procedure that the Zapruder material had to undergo when the US government tried to reconstruct what happened on Dealy Plaza in Dallas on 22 November 1963. Just as the single images of the 8mm film were blown up to disclose the mystery of the Kennedy assassination, Thomas tries to find an explanation for the mysterious events in the park.[153]

The process of enlargement provides Thomas's investigation with further visual information, enabling him to make visible former invisible details, such as the face, the pistol and the corpse. It almost seems as if he can go beneath the surface of the visual image, thus gaining access to deeper, hitherto hidden layers of reality.[154] Ultimately, however, the larger the images become the less clear the contours of the object in question will be. Due to the material nature of photographs the grain on the print becomes larger every time and, consequently, less will be visible in the image.

---

[152] This experience is shared by the audience (when watching the film for the first time). Although the body is there at the end of the park scene, the spectator will not discover it until the protagonist detects it on his photograph.

[153] According to *Village Voice* (December 1991) three early reviews drew a connection between the murder mystery of *Blow-Up* and the assassination of JFK and its coincidental recording on film by the amateur Abraham Zapruder. Nicolas Schröder, "Blow-Up" in *50 Klassiker Film. Die Wichtigsten Werke der Filmgeschichte* (Hildesheim: Gerstenberg, 2000), 180-182

[154] In this respect, the photographic picture also seems to function like a palimpsest as the 'different' traces of light on the image resemble the various inscriptions on the parchment.

The largest image Thomas produces is a triple blow-up of the corpse. He produces it by taking another photograph of a detail on one of the blow-ups with a large-format camera. As a result, he finds the former image decomposed into an abstract grey-in-grey structured pattern, which, when he puts it on an easel, resembles his friend Bill's abstract paintings.[155] As the only picture left in the photographer's studio after the burglary, it almost seems to mock him. Deprived of the context provided by the other photographs, it has lost its meaning and become useless as evidence of the crime.[156]

The photograph as a simulacrum

The triple blow-up Thomas has produced is not a representation of reality but a representation of a representation. It lacks reference in the dual sense when both the image that served as its source in production and the body in the park as real reference for the latter have disappeared. It can therefore be argued that the single remaining abstract blow-up has turned into a mere simulacrum as it has become an empty sign without meaning. It does not even represent an image, since, devoid of reference, it represents nothing. Ultimately, the triple blow-up functions as an image of the medium as such.

Throughout the protagonist's visual investigation, photography is unmasked as an insufficient representation of reality. As the image is merely a surface, its revelatory qualities are limited. The photographer is not able to make more things visible than had been before. From a certain point of enlargement the process of realization is reversed, and the details that have become clear through focus gradually vanish again until they are no longer recognizable.

Photographic narrative

As the photographic scenes from the park have been removed from their former temporal and causal context, Thomas stands before his photographic material and cannot find a coherent meaning in it. The detected clues do not fit into the romantic image of the love scene, and he needs to find an

---

[155] In this respect Thomas's investigation moves in a contrary direction to his neighbour's interpretations of his abstract paintings: the alleged obvious meaning is challenged and subverted into another meaning before all meaning is lost in the remaining abstract blow-up.

[156] It seems as if the image had been forgotten by the 'thieves'. It can also be interpreted as a mockery, however, left there deliberately to tell him that it was none of his business.

alternative interpretation as explanation. He finally finds a way out of this "epistemological aporia or impasse" by creating a photographic narrative.[157] By reassembling the black and white images of his park scene into a coherent narrative sequence the photographer simultaneously interprets the given material and creates a new context, thus endowing the images with significance.[158]

As Thomas "is creating a temporal continuum out of a series of still images", thus attempting to offset their stillness, the blow-up scene again resembles the act of film making.[159] As the protagonist's interpretive gaze travels along the chronology of the photographic narrative in the form of the subjective camera, the images appear to be the shots of a silent film.

In the blow-up scene, Thomas functions as director, cameraman and editor (as well as viewer) of the film within the film. Where Hitchcock's protagonist applies the use of binoculars and telephoto lens, Antonioni's photographer provides the film with different shot sizes (close-up shots) using blow-ups of the details.[160]

In the blow-up scene, however, the focus is laid on the significance of the connection between the given pieces of visual information in order to create meaning (and, thus, determine the interpretation). The single images become a photographic narrative by applying the principles of montage theory, which is essentially based on the underlying assumption that "everything is dependent on a particular context for its significance".[161] As Thomas stands in front of two images with his head (as viewed from the audience's perspective) and thoughts (from his own point of view) constituting the link between them, his mind creates a connection between the single images, thereby producing a context from whose origin a meaning grows: the murder. With the gun in the bushes, as climax of the

---

[157] Colin Gardner: *Antonioni's Blow-Up and the Chiasmus of Memory.* http://www.artbrain.org/journal2/gardner.html (25 July 2010)

[158] Thus, through his photographic narrative Thomas's creative act as composer of images is reversed. Usually, artificial 'realities' come into being in his studio before (or while) he releases the button of his camera. This time, the creative part follows the shooting. Brunette points out with reference to Juri Lotman (in "Les problèmes de la sémiotique et les voies du cinéma contemporain", 173-174) that Thomas's process of operation resembles "the work of the semiotician who cuts up representations into units (like the blow-ups), then considers them as signs to be deciphered, using both the paradigmatic and syntagmatic axes". Brunette, 174

[159] Boyd, 37

[160] For a reading of the blow-up scene as metaphor for film making see also Robert T. Eberwein, "The Master Text of *Blow-Up*" (*Close Viewings*), 275

[161] Boyd, 41

photographic narrative, the crime emerges out of his photographic material and within the photographer's logic of interpretation.[162]

While he is trying to get the pictures into the 'correct' order Thomas is again distracted. The erotic episode with the teenage girls, however, finally directs the photographer towards the pivotal clue of the full explanation of what happened in the park. As Gerard Oppermann points out, Thomas's own undressing leads him to the next clue: he must himself lie on the floor of his studio like a dead person (after the erotic turbulences) to discover the dead body lying on the ground in the bright space on the blow-up before his eyes.[163]

To examine his discovery, the photographer compares the full shots of the park scenery before and after his encounter with the woman (thus resembling Jeffries comparing the slides of the flowerbed in the backyard) and marks the bright spot on the ground beneath the tree in the middle of the lawn.

The meaning of the images therefore changes again: they have become the visual evidence of a murder. His former expectations of the romantic idyll of the park, with its natural atmosphere of peacefulness as the scenario for the joyful game of two lovers, have been completely disappointed. Instead, his images have turned into the documentation of the site of a crime. There is menace and danger lurking in the bushes. And the unconscious preventer of a murder is turned into the unconscious witness who unwittingly documented the crime.

---

[162] According to Béla Balász in "Theory of The Film" the blow-ups of the details, which resemble close-up shots in a (silent) film, widen and deepen Thomas's vision of the events, revealing new things (head, pistol, corpse) and showing the meaning of the old (the 'normal-size' blow-ups). See Leo Braudy and Marshall Cohen, eds. *Film Theory and Criticism. Introductory Readings* (New York and Oxford: Oxford University Press, 1999), 304

[163] Gerard Oppermann, "Die Mittelszene des Filmes *Blow-Up*" (*Michelangelo Antonioni*), 29-34. Stoermer argues, however, that due to a suggestive pan of the camera, which seems to be emancipated from the protagonist's gaze, the spectator must have already noticed the corpse on the blow-up before the photographer discovers it after the sexual interlude. This resembles the viewer's 'privileged' view of the woman in the black dress whom Hitchcock's protagonist misses in *Rear Window*. See Stoermer, http://www.nachdemfilm.de/content/unschuldige-beweise

Photographic paranoia and epistemological confusion

Seeking to verify the suspicions emerging from the narrative of his photographic material (does he not trust his images as representations of reality?), Thomas returns to the park at night. As he is too confused, he forgets to take his 'instrument to master reality'.[164]

When he sees the corpse actually lying on the ground - it is the woman's older lover - and even touches it, the images are replaced by real experience. On his return to the studio, he finds it in a mess: the evidence has disappeared, the negatives and images have been stolen - except for the triple blow-up. He therefore meets his friend Ron to take him to the park to see the corpse. He also wants to make up for the photograph he could not take. Distracted by the party, however, and his friend being too stoned to understand, Thomas ends up boozing the night away.

It is not until the next morning that the photographer carries out his intention. This time, equipped with his camera, he finds himself deceived again as the corpse has disappeared. It has thus become impossible to verify the murder by means of another image.

As Peter Brunette points out, "reality is always unconsciously constructed and all reality and all meaning are achieved contextually, by means of the frame around a given bit of reality".[165] This means that perception is not "a solitary act but performed within a particular community and it is shaped and constrained by the communal ideology".[166]

There are several symbolic illustrations of this idea in the film. Torn out of their actual context, the propeller and the piece of the broken guitar, for example, lose their former significance. In this respect the mimes, whose appearance at the beginning and at the end provides a frame for the film, function as an "emblem of the social construction of reality".[167] They symbolize a group that has agreed on a certain way of perceiving the world. When Thomas returns the invisible ball at the end of the film, his participation in the game means that he "accepts the authority of this group to name meaning and thus configure reality".[168]

---

[164] See Robert T. Eberwein, "The Master Text of *Blow-Up*" (*Close Viewings*), 278

[165] Brunette, 117

[166] Boyd, 40

[167] Boyd, 47

[168] Brunette, 117. Eberwein describes the mimes' tennis match as working like a *mise en abyme* within the text of the film "as a comment on its own operations". Robert T. Eberwein, "The Master Text of *Blow-Up*" (*Close Viewings*), 279

Thus, with photography as a "mechanism for the sharing of perception" and medium of artistic communication undermined, the protagonist lacks a kindred spirit with whom to share his knowledge.[169] As a result, Thomas's need for verification of his interpretation of reality remains unsatisfied.

In an age where seeing is believing and images confirm the truth, he has no proof of his suspicion. Since all the visual evidence has dissolved into nothing, the murder seems to be no longer real. With the corpse gone too, the crime merely exists within the photographer's own visual memory. Therefore, at the end of the film, Thomas, thrown back upon himself, seems to be as uncertain about the credibility of the murder as about the reliability of photography as representation of reality.

4. A reality is a reality is a reality...

Thomas as a postmodern voyeur

As a member of the 'Beat Generation' in the Swinging London of the Sixties, Antonioni's hip young photographer is not merely representative of the emancipation of a young generation leaving behind old-fashioned norms and values. Denzin identifies him as another early postmodern voyeur. As the life-style of the society he belongs to is characterized by superficiality, however, "it can no longer be assumed that the voyeur will answer to a higher good".[170] Although the photographer becomes a detective whose investigation leads to the disclosure of a murder, Thomas does not act out of moral duty. Unlike Hitchcock's voyeur, he is not interested in handing a murderer over to the police. His investigation is not as much concerned with the murder as with the significance of his photographic material.

Denzin, therefore, reads *Blow-Up* as a critique of a visual society that bases its assumptions about reality on visual representation. The film deconstructs the visual field, which merely captures surface appearances and technological apparatuses - the photographic camera (and the film camera) - that bring it into play.[171]

Blow-Up therefore also touches on Debord's term of the 'society of the spectacle'. It can be argued that it concludes with the realization that reality cannot be 'mastered' by images since it eludes representation. Accordingly, the film also seems to state that reality cannot be grasped by mere visual perception, but that it must also be confronted, as appearances can be deceptive.

---

[169] Boyd, 40

[170] Denzin, *Cinematic Society*, 137

[171] Denzin, *Cinematic Society*, 135

In this respect, *Blow-Up* also anticipates the postmodern notion of the simulacrum. As the photographic images change their meaning, their status as representations shifts from a sign concealing the truth (love scene instead of murder) to a sign that is a copy of a non-existent reality (the abstract triple blow-up devoid of context and reference).[172]

Blow-Up as postmodern 'master text'

Although the film's protagonist has come close to solving the mystery, the case remains unresolved. Unlike Jeffries, Antonioni's photographer is not able to verify his suspicion of murder (which implies both his assumption about reality as well as the meaning/interpretation of his photographic material). Despite the fact that his first return to the park reveals the 'truth' of his suspicion when he discovers the corpse, reality eludes his attempt to 'master' it by means of representation. On his return to record this 'truth' on film, the corpse has disappeared (and all photographic evidence too). Thus, - in contrast to *Rear Window* - visual paranoia in *Blow-Up* does not conclude with an objective truth or reality.

Since it does not provide a definite solution for the murder mystery, the film, too, cannot be mastered by a definite interpretation. Robert T. Eberwein therefore describes *Blow-Up* as an early postmodern 'master text'.[173] The diegetic content and the use of the self-reflexive narrative structure in *Blow-Up* reflect the postmodern endeavour to permanently interpret or reinterpret; an aspect that also finds expression in cultural paranoia. The film seems to conclude with the postmodern notion of the subject and society being in constant doubt concerning the question of whether there is an 'objective' reality that can be represented as true or false; the notion that it is impossible to decide on the validity of either this or that meaning or the 'truth'. The film rather seems to promote the belief that there are various, maybe even an endless number of co-existing realities as well as images of reality, each depending on the context and one's point of view.

Finally, *Blow-Up* is a master text on the mystery of images. This aspect, however, is not only reflected within the film's diegetic content but also on a meta-level. The photographer's mastery over his environment and his domination of the imaginary is turned into subservience (as in the mimes'

---

[172] See the four stages of the image as described by Jean Baudrillard in "The Precession of Simulacra" (in *Simulations*, 1983), *Postmodernism. A Reader*, ed. Thomas Docherty (New York: Pearson Education, 2003), 196

[173] Robert T. Eberwein, "The Master Text of *Blow-Up*" (*Close Viewings*), 262

mute tennis match). The protagonist, at the end of the film, decomposes like the corpse on his blow-ups.[174]

Taylor points out a relationship between 'conspiracy' as part of the plot and the conspiracy of the film as a narrative. Accordingly, there is a structural similarity between the conspirator and the film maker.[175] In this respect, through 'Antonioni's autograph' at the end of the film the protagonist's status as an element in the plot is emphasized, and both the film's and the film maker's conspiracy are unmasked.[176] As "a hero in a narrative that determines and speaks him as a signifier",[177] he has no control over what happens to him.[178]

---

[174] ibidem, 263, 270

[175] Taylor, 49

[176] Seymour Chatman, "*Il provino* and *Blow-Up*" in *Antonioni or The Surface of the World* (Berkeley, Los Angeles, London: UCP, 1985), 145

[177] Robert T. Eberwein, "The Master Text of *Blow-Up*" (*Close Viewings*), 278

[178] This is a forecast of 'Agency Panic' (Melley), which will be discussed in detail later with reference to *The Truman Show*.

5. The photographic paranoia plot in *Blow-Up*

The paranoia plot in *Blow-Up* begins with the park scene. The photographer happens to encounter a couple – a young woman and an obviously older man. Instantly the idea arises of catching some soothing pictures for the closing chapter of his documentary book on London.

Thomas follows the couple from a distance, secretly observing their philandering.

He hides behind the fence to take some pictures.

The photographer creeps forward taking a zigzag course, hiding behind the trees and secretly taking more close-up pictures of the assumed intimacy between these lovebirds.

Suddenly, the woman has become aware that the photographer is following them and, very upset, she runs towards him. She demands that he surrenders the film immediately.

She seems to be completely beside herself, even biting the photographer's hand to force him to give her the film.

When Thomas stays put, she suddenly runs away, stopping after a while for a moment, with Thomas taking pictures of her, until she leaves the scene. The man with whom she has been flirting has disappeared.

After meeting his friend, the publisher of his London book, he noticed from the window of the café someone meddling around at his car. Thomas returns home to be confronted by the woman from the park, who had arrived there at the same time.

Since she has come for the film, she tries to steal the camera when Thomas is momentarily distracted. The attempt fails. Thomas catches her in the act.

Desperately wanting to get the film roll, she is more or less prepared to reciprocate the favour with some hanky-panky if necessary. It seems that Thomas is responding to her feminine charms. He finally gives her the film – at least what she believes to be *the* film. In his darkroom he has removed the film from the camera, and returns he with a substitute film.

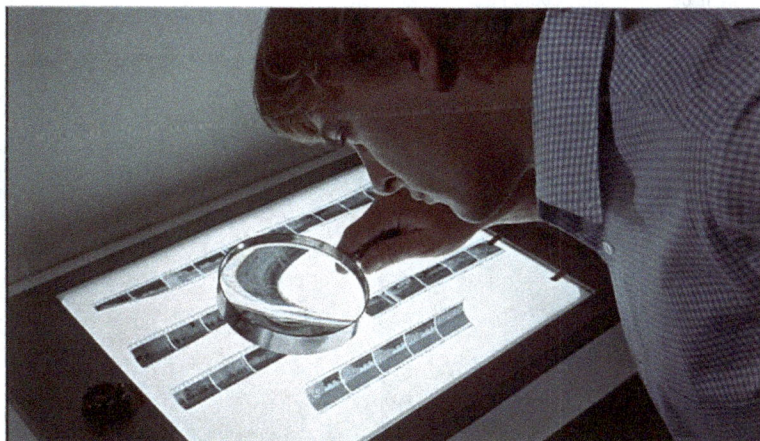

As soon as the woman has left Thomas develops the film material. The woman's visit and her weird behaviour have aroused the photographer's curiosity. The investigation begins: the photographer searches the negatives for some visual information about the strange affair.

Having picked out the most meaningful frames, Thomas develops the prints, which he blows up very large. He pins them to his studio walls and scrutinizes them thoroughly. By screening the photographic material he wants to find a reason for the woman's discomposure concerning the scene in the park and being observed and documented. There is a vague suspicion of something beyond the obvious.

Thomas questions the pictures and tries to make sense of the visual signs the material holds. He scrutinizes to every detail, every gesture, every glance that might be a sign that could help him solve the mystery.

The woman's gaze on the photo showing the couple embracing and hugging catches Thomas's eye.

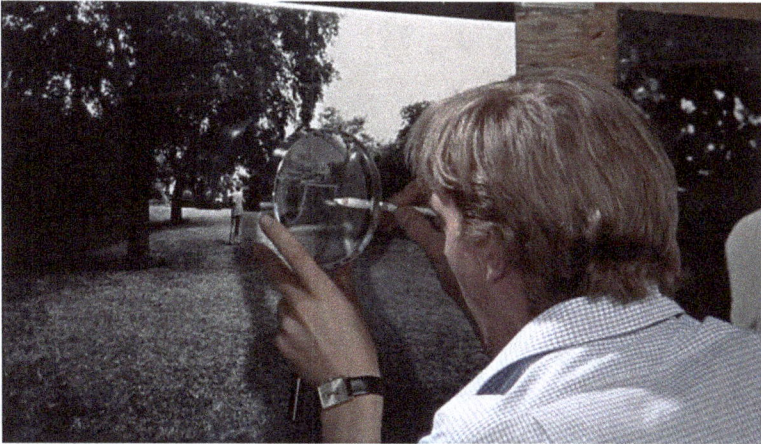

Following the direction of the woman's gaze, Thomas' attention is drawn to a spot not to be deciphered by the naked eye – although using a magnifying glass as technical support. He marks the spot to produce another blow-up.

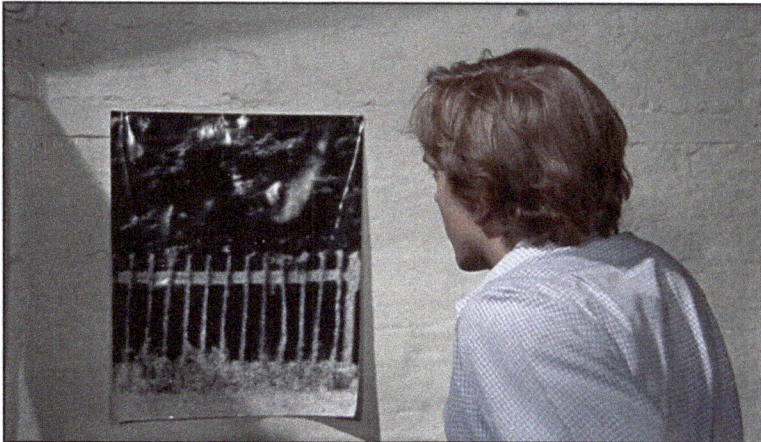

What he gets is a detail of the face of a man peering through the bushes behind the fence. He does not yet understand, however, what the sequence is adding up to. He remembers having asked for the girl's phone number and wants to ring her up – a blind end, since she has given him a false number.

He tries to hit on an idea himself. Staring at the images, he suddenly has a clue. He rushes into the darkroom to make another blow-up.

The blow-up discloses a man with a revolver in the bushes behind the fence to which the woman's gaze had been directed.

Now the bits and pieces need to be arranged (anew). The clues and details have to be woven into a coherent context. Thomas arranges the prints on the walls of his studio in a chronological order, which makes sense to him - with the blow-ups highlighting the formerly missed details. He thus produces a visual narrative (like a storyboard) of the secret plot he had innocently witnessed.

At this point, he is all of a tizzy and calls his friend Ron to tell him he that he saved somebody's life. - However, after the hanky-panky with the teenage girls, Thomas comes to the conclusion that he has not yet got the right storyline.

He thoroughly re-examines the material and compares the images of the park before and after the intermezzo with the upset woman.

He hangs on to a detail that brings about a metamorphosis of the park scene. He finds that with his naked eyes and his 'naive' camera view he has misinterpreted the scene at first sight: the former assumption of an innocent and intimate love scene turns into the disclosure of a crime.

In his darkroom he produces a detailed blow-up from the initial blow-up.

The result is two blow-ups, one grainier than the other, resembling a body lying on the lawn; the body of the older man lying at the place where the girl had stopped for an instance before running off.

These pictures finally tip the scales: Thomas detects a murder and becomes a witness of it.

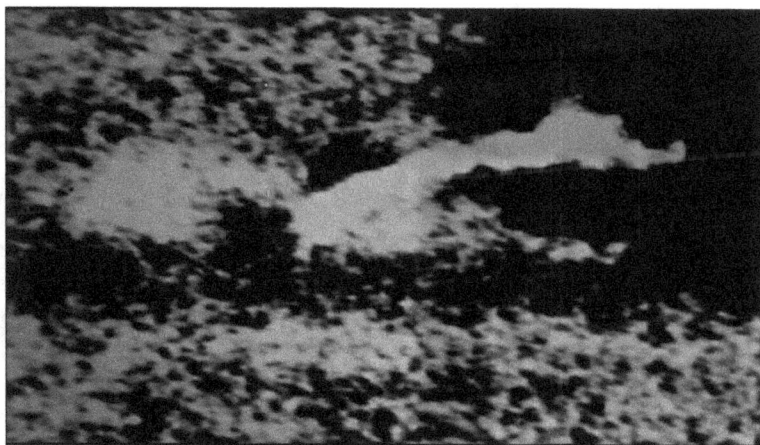

The photographic material enabled Thomas to turn back time and get immersed in the morning scene in the park. On examining the photographs Thomas found a network of interrelated signs, which had been invisible to the naked eye. The photographic chain of evidence culminates in the crucial blow-up resembling an almost distorted close-up of the dead body.

The verification of the photographic evidence: After his detection of the crime by means of the photographic material the photographer returns to the park at night – to find the dead 'corpus delicti'.

The man is still lying where Thomas found him on the grainy prints. Unexpectedly, however, Thomas had forgotten to bring along his camera to record this moment with another close-up of the corpse at night.

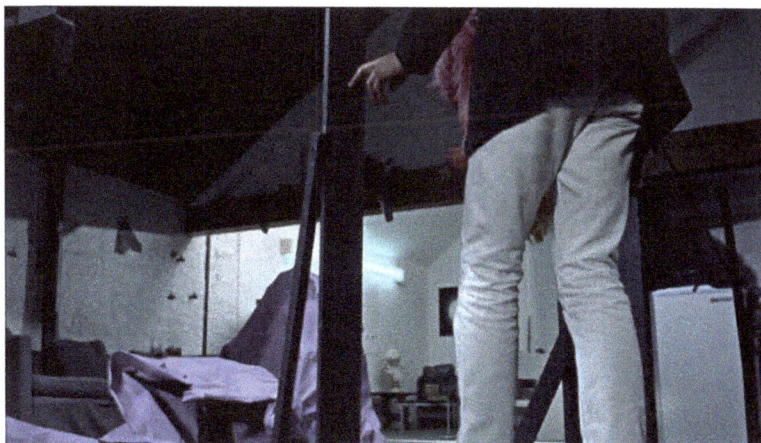

When the photographer returns home he finds his studio ransacked. All the prints and all negative materials have been stolen.

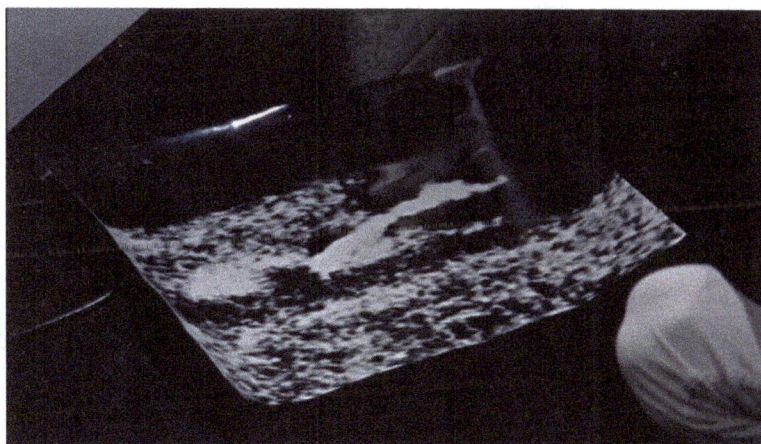

The only remaining evidence is the rough-grained fuzzy blow-up of the body, which had fallen between the furniture. Because of its distortion beyond recognition it is merely an obscure sign that, deprived of its former context, has lost its significance (similar to the discarded broken guitar from the *Yardbirds* concert).

Thomas then phones Ron, whom he then meets at a party, where everybody seems to be on drugs, to take him to the park to witness the scene and get a shot of the body. - On his way to the party he had seen the girl from the park among passers-by. He tried to follow her, but got lost in a club where the *Yardbirds* were giving a concert.)

When the photographer returns to the park again the next morning, after the party, the body has disappeared. Thomas fails to take the crucial picture with which he might have attested the crime.

Alone in the park, this time with his camera, the photographer finds himself deprived of both his spectacular story and the visual power of the photographic image. Since the pictures - which a few hours ago had the relevance to help him reveal a murder – are gone, what really transpired in the park has now turned into a blurred memory...

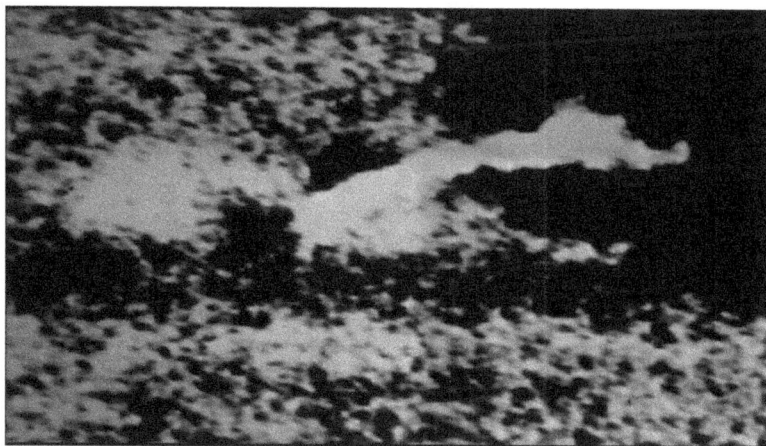

The single remaining image back at his studio does not substantiate anything; it does not mean anything. Thomas is baffled.

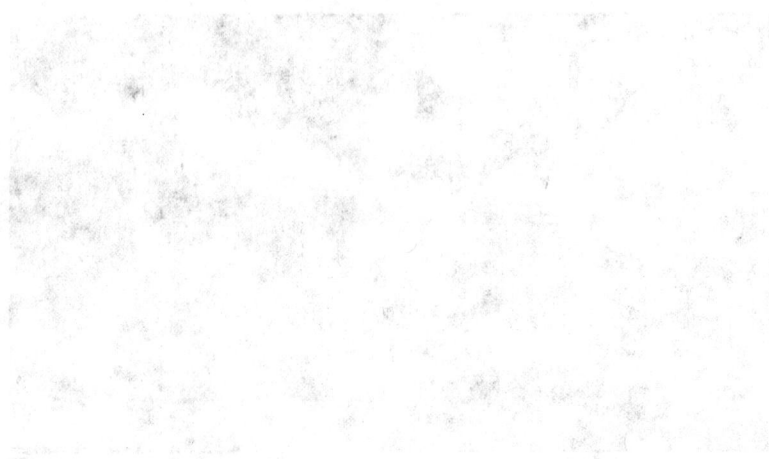

IV. SCOPOPHOBIC PARANOIA IN THE TRUMAN SHOW

1. A multi-layered reality

> "Modernity, wherever it appears, does not
> occur without a shattering of belief, without a
> discovery of the lack of reality in reality – a
> discovery linked to the invention of other
> realities."
>
> J.-F. Lyotard in: *An Introduction to Visual Culture*, 7

> "To live in postmodernity is to live constantly
> under the gaze of an all-seeing eye, gathering
> information about us."
>
> Bran Nicol, *Reading Paranoia*, 45

Narrative structure

Peter Weir's *The Truman Show* (1998) is a cinematic text with typical postmodernist features regarding both its contents and narrative structure. The film contains several intertextual links and, with the setting located pastiche-like in the 1950s, it also touches on the Jamesonian term of the nostalgia film.[179] *The Truman Show* uses the conventions of television, blurring the genres of reality TV, soap opera, talk show, documentary and commercial advertising. Within an intricate, self-reflexive film-within-film structure it creates several levels of reality and various layers of meaning.

The narrative contains three textual levels that are cleverly interlocked. On the diegetic level, Weir's film is about the last days of a world-famous American non-stop live TV programme: Christof's *Truman Show* is a real-life docusoap about the life of its unwitting star Truman Burbank. Accordingly, on the hypodiegetic level the film is concerned with the dawning awareness of the unwitting star of *The Truman Show* that he might not be the man he thought he was. Or rather, he finds himself trapped in a reality that does

---

[179] Michael Kokonis has traced the references of *The Truman Show* to several other films that are alluded to in various ways. He mentions among other examples Truman's reaction to the stage light dropping from the sky, which can be seen as a reminiscence of the apes examining the mysterious slab in Kubrick's *2001: A Space Odyssey*. The repetitive pattern of Truman's everyday routine and rituals inevitably reminds us of *Groundhog Day*, and the Seahaven extras in the show resemble the 'alienated' human beings in Carpenter's films *They Live* and the *Invasion of the Body Snatchers*. Michael Kokonis, "Postmodernism, Hyperreality and the Hegemony of Spectacle in New Hollywood: The Case of *The Truman Show*" in *Gramma. Periodiko Theorias Kai Kritikes* No. 7 (Thessaloniki, 1999), 63-66. (For the last example see also O'Donnell, 1-10; and Pratt, 240.) I will comment on the aspect of nostalgia in *The Truman Show* later.

not really exist, where he is being manipulated to behave as a normal guy. In this respect, the narrative within the narrative is a coming-of-age story of a thirty year old man who has been kept in an unconscious state of dependency, and who manages to escape his panoptic life. And finally, the third textual level is devoted to the on-screen viewers of Christof's *Truman Show*. As representatives of the worldwide TV audience, they function as a mirror to the off-screen audience. As a result of this reflective effect, the viewer of *The Truman Show* is linked to its narrative in a peculiar way. He is simultaneously drawn into and absorbed by the narrative and, at the same time, he is kept at a distance and made aware of his perceptive status as cinematic voyeur.[180]

Narrative perspective

The hypodiegetic narrative of the show, which constitutes most of the film, is mainly presented through shots from unusual or extreme camera angles. The latter are intended to simulate the spying gaze of the 5000 hidden cameras around Seahaven Island. As a result the spectator becomes a panoptic voyeur. He shares the surveilling gaze effected by the film crew in the moon control room, which is also the perspective shared by the on-screen audience.

The spectator is, however, not merely made an accomplice of the voyeurs. From the beginning of the film, with Christof and the actors who play Meryl and Marlon commenting on the show in the first 'documentary' shots intercut with the opening titles of the show, the audience is initiated into the 'conspiracy'. As the film's self-reflexive structure provides visual knowledge about the diegetic real world outside the show, too, it also renders the spectator a voyeur of voyeurs. Thus, the spectator is able to look behind the scenes, seeing shots of the control room where Christof and his team are pulling the strings of the show. The audience's dual voyeurism also includes the viewers of the on-screen audience in front of their television screens watching the show all over the world.

The audience is thus in the privileged position of a multi-angular perspective, which induces a sense of the dual reality from the very beginning. As a result, they gradually realize that there is another meaning to several incidents; for example, when in the hypodiegetic narrative actors sometimes suddenly step out of line. For an instant, the hidden layer of the diegetic reality shimmers through the surface of the show reality. The spectator therefore knows why Truman was prevented from climbing up the rocks on the beach as a small boy, that the voice in the car's radio is communicating only with Truman, that the bus driver apologizes to him

---

[180] In this respect, it might be argued that the off-screen audience constitutes a further meta-diegetic level.

personally for his failure and that the little girl on the bus almost blabs out that she knows Truman from the TV show. When Truman and Meryl cross the bridge despite the warning, and she cries that they are not allowed to do this, the spectator knows also that she does not merely mean because of the sign, but because she knows that the bridge leads towards the exit of the Seahaven dome. The same 'conspiratorial knowledge' applies to the commercials that are woven into the story.[181]

Despite the viewer's multi-dimensional perspective and his superior voyeuristic position the narrative only reveals the true nature of Truman's existence slowly. In this respect, both the structure of the film and the experience of film reception reflect the gradual emergence of the protagonist's suspicion. While Truman collects the pieces of the puzzle that make up the truth about his life, the viewer simultaneously gathers pieces of information that expose the full dimension of the conspiracy behind Truman's being.[182] Accordingly, the film's narrative structure affects the viewer: he does not merely observe what happens, but to some extent becomes absorbed by Truman's paranoia. Finally, as the mystery surrounding Truman's destiny dissolves, the film's initial comic lightness increasingly turns into grotesque tragedy.

2. A postmodern condition: hyperreality and panopticism

The protagonist of *The Truman Show* is not only a signifier in the signifying chain of the cinematic text that is Weir's film. Truman, as his name suggests is the only real person in a non-stop television spectacle. He is a narrative element in a dual sense, operating on both the meta level as well as within the diegesis of the film. He is the main character in someone else's story, the unwitting star of a real-life docusoap, created and directed by Christof.

From the embryo stage in his mother's womb, Truman has been secretly observed and recorded. He was adopted by the film company as an unborn child and grew up to be a man in the largest film studio in the world. For almost thirty years, Truman's life has been broadcast live on TV.

Completely innocent of the fact that his life is merely a show, Truman appears to be a true 'Everyman'. All his perceptions are, however, based on

---

[181] With reference to *Rear Window* I find that there are several allusions to 'women in black dresses', which the protagonist is not capable of understanding as long as he is completely innocent.

[182] This aspect becomes clear with the scene in which his best friend, Marlon, is talking to the increasingly confused Truman. The audience is taken aback (at least that is how I felt about it) by the revelation that the intimate conversation is being controlled from above with Christof whispering the actor's text word by word into his ear.

unreal premises. He merely lives Christof's illusion of the average life of an ordinary person, determined by job routine and repetition.[183]

Lost in simulation

Truman is the only authentic part in a world characterized by the hyperreal. Reminiscent of the Platonian parable of the cave, Seahaven Island can be read as a simulation. According to Baudrillard's terminology, the setting of the show shifts between the third and fourth stage of simulation.[184] On the one hand, the self-contained artificial world beneath a giant dome with the illusion of the sky projected onto the roof of the dome, the computer-based programmes for daylight and weather, and the detached houses in pastel colours, which give Seahaven the impression of a simulated Disneyland-like commercial town, conceals the absence of reality.[185] On the other hand, however, the place can at the same time be described as a simulacrum. Completely secluded from the outside world, it is a reality in which things are not what they seem. It is made up of empty signs, a universe of superficial appearances. Thus the real is not merely absent, it is replaced by the hyperreal.

In this fake world the most real element is the identikit portrait of the protagonist's true love. It is a collage put together from scraps torn out of a fashion magazine that he secretly hides on the reverse side of his wife's photograph, locked up in a wooden chest. Paradoxically, the fake picture - which is much more symbolic of a simulacrum in the dual sense (that is, a simulacrum composed of simulacra) - is the only sign in this world of false appearances that has a true deeper meaning. Despite its dissimilarity, it has a hidden reference to reality (the girl he really loves). It is the only thing that has real significance for Truman. He takes it with him when he steps into the real world.

Not only is Truman's life and environment a simulation, the people surrounding him in this world are also fake. All of Seahaven's inhabitants

---

[183] See Margaret Rogersons elaborations on *The Truman Show* read as postmodern everyman narrative. Margaret Rogerson, "The Truman Show: An Everyman for the Late 1990s" in *Sydney Studies in English* No. 26 (Sydney, N.S.W., 2000), 25-44.

[184] Jean Baudrillard in "The Precession of Simulacra" (in *Simulations*, 1983) as referred to in *Postmodernism. A Reader*, ed. Thomas Docherty (New York: Pearson Education, 2003), 196. As Pratt also remarks, Truman's realization reflects the philosophical tradition rooted in Plato's allegory of the cave that finally "anticipated the world of mass-media image construction [and - more recent still - the world of computer-generated images]". Pratt, 239, 240

[185] Baudrillard mentions Disneyland as an example of a third-order simulation. See Peter Barry, *Beginning Theory. An Introduction to Literary and Cultural Theory* (Manchester and New York: Manchester University Press, 1995), 88-89

are actors and actresses, including his neighbours, colleagues and even his wife, mother and best friend Marlon. The living characters of Truman's staged life, they are given stage directions via radio contact to perform scripted events and enact seemingly realistic situations to effect the dramaturgy of Truman's soap opera life.

Visibility as a trap

The Truman Show draws on the notion of the postmodern as characterized by panopticism in Michel Foucault's sense. In Weir's film, the protagonist appears to be the object of the gaze.

As his life is a TV show, every move Truman makes is secretly recorded, ready to be broadcast. Even when he is asleep he is live on air. In order to be able to watch him continually, the world Truman lives in resembles a postmodern media-sustained panopticon, where the camera world of surveillance and broadcasting merge.[186] Seahaven is a surveillance complex in which control of the architectonic panopticon is shifted onto a level of image-based captivity through establishing a huge network of cameras. The entire set and the actors are equipped with 5000 hidden cameras, through which the panoptic gaze is put into operation. They are connected to the monitors in the control room high up in the moon, which, not least through its transformation into a searchlight towards the end of the film, resembles a panoptic tower. As a technical image strategy, the constant invisible supervision can be transferred to all spheres of Truman's life, providing a 'radical visibility'.[187]

Panopticism in *The Truman Show* becomes an ambiguous dimension, as the empty gaze of the surveillance cameras encompasses two kinds of gazes. The disguised appearance of the panopticon ensures the panoptic gaze is not merely invisible to Truman, but that the object of its gaze is completely unaware of his surveillance. As a result, his permanent visibility enables the 'man in the moon' to control and manipulate Truman's life without his knowledge, while it simultaneously satisfies the voyeuristic desire of the on-screen TV audience. As the latter watches the show for its entertainment, Truman, seen from their point of view, resembles not a prisoner in his cell but much more an animal trapped in a cage. Thus, the

---

[186] Manfred Faßler, *Bildlichkeit - Navigationen durch das Repertoire der Sichtbarkeit* (Wien, Köln, Weimar: Böhlau, 2002), 54

[187] Pauleit points out that in a society in which nothing can exist without illustration - visual culture - the panopticon has established itself on the level of technical images through closed-circuit TV. Winfried Pauleit, „Videoüberwachung und postmoderne Subjekte. Ein Hypertext zu den Facetten einer Bildmaschine" in *Nach dem Film* No 3: *Video und Überwachung* (01/10/2001); http://www.nachdemfilm.de/content/no-3-video-und-überwachung (14 August 2010)

panoptic system in *The Truman Show* not only resembles Bentham's prison model, it is also an image of Le Vau's ménagerie, also mentioned by Foucault in this context.[188]

3. Scopophobic paranoia

Truman's life is characterized by repetition and predictability. This pattern is only interrupted when things suddenly happen that increasingly challenge his acceptance of the surrounding world. Small mistakes creep in, causing visible ruptures on the surface of this fabricated world, and gradually the seamlessness of the illusion begins to crumble. By bumping into the boundaries of his television world he stumbles over the true nature of its falseness. The character of his life as a stage production becomes increasingly visible, and Truman finally discovers the hidden agenda behind his televisual existence. He slowly realizes that he is being watched in order to be controlled and contained.

Delusions of grandeur and persecution

The first crack in Christof's 'master plan' is Truman's one and only true encounter in his scripted life. The incident is cut into the show as a flashback, when Truman seems to remember the girl after trying to improve his identikit picture of her. Lauren/Sylvia tried to reveal her true identity to the college student he then was, as well as the unbelievable truth about his existence.

In removing her from the show, Christof manages to re-establish order and routine in Truman's life, and the latter unwittingly follows the plan of his television destiny by getting married to the importunate Meryl. The puzzling incident with the girl he has fallen in love with, however, induces a diffuse, latent doubt in Truman. This exciting experience in his otherwise monotonous life has led him to unconsciously question whether the life in Seahaven is really all there is to his existence.

A floodlight falling from the sky is the next mysterious incident that irritates the protagonist's view of his world. Disturbing Truman's everyday morning ritual, the technical error is the first visible clue of a hidden reality in the emergence of his paranoia. This strange occurrence, the effects of which are reduced by a news flash about an alleged plane accident, is soon followed by rainfall, like a shower, that selectively pours down on him and follows him wherever he goes. His amused astonishment about this, however, gradually becomes the realization that he is living in "Trumania in

---

[188] For Foucault's description of Bentham's panopticon (the text also includes a description of Le Vau's ménagerie) see Foucault, 256-261

the Burbank galaxy", where everything revolves around him.[189] In this world, traffic immediately stops to save his life - no matter how unpredictably he rushes into the street - and even policemen unknown to him know his name. Everyone seems to be informed about Truman's actions and intentions. His wife, for instance, knows about the encounter with his father, the 'lift-accident' and his attempt to book a flight to Fiji before he tells her.

Truman's diffuse suspicions turn into the assumption that he is under surveillance when, one morning, on his way to work, there is a sudden shift in the frequency of the radio programme he is listening to. A voice from the control centre passes on information about his route, and when the mistake is noticed a piercing sound causes Truman's surrounding environment to freeze. For a moment, life outside his car seems to have come to a complete standstill - as if the clockwork of the world stops - only to continue the next instant as if nothing had happened. Completely taken aback, Truman eventually figures out that something is going on around him, of which he is the target, and that all the people in the street must be involved in this conspiracy against him.

From this moment on, Truman no longer believes the explanation of the voice in the radio claiming the mistake was caused by a momentary jamming of the frequency by the police radio. Lost in confusion and full of mistrust he looks around the place, searching for visible clues to gain an insight into the wheelings and dealings behind the scenes. Having noticed a suspicious-looking person, Truman departs from his usual way to work and follows him into the lobby of a corporate building. There he experiences the ultimate 'eye opener' of the dual reality around him: hidden behind the façade of a lift's door he catches a glimpse of the backstage area of the show.[190]

Truman turns detective

Truman's gaze beyond the limits of his former reality awakens a kind of visual paranoia in him that causes him to doubt everything he sees. From now on he takes nothing for granted. Taking a solipsistic view of life around him, he starts observing his environment with heightened awareness for inconsistencies.[191]

In the course of his visual investigation Truman discovers that the alleged normal life around him is not as normal as he thought. In time he becomes

---

[189] This is what he tells his mirror image in the bathroom one morning.

[190] Kokonis, 64

[191] Pratt, 239

aware that the world around him is a stage and that those who act on it are merely players.[192]

Putting the people in a supermarket to a test, Truman finds out that he cannot behave crazily enough to make them pay attention to him. They seem to be mere 'pod people', incapable of a 'normal' human reaction. Another example of this behaviour occurs when the passengers of a Chicago bus leave the vehicle meekly, without grumbling, even though the driver has turned out to be a duffer.[193] Truman, moreover, realizes that life around him is not only too quiet, but also too predictable to be true. While secretly observing the scenery and movements where he lives through the rear-view mirror of his car, he discovers that the same actors continually reappear. At this point, Truman is not merely the 'observed', he himself becomes a conscious observer.

An even greater shock is the discovery that the commercial-drivelling Meryl is not really his wife, when he sees her crossed fingers on their wedding picture with the help of a magnifying glass. After this breathtaking revelation the deceived husband 'secretly' follows the woman - who pretends to love him – to 'work', to gain more information on her suspected conspiratorial doings. The cast manages, however, to scrape through the situation by giving the appearance of a hospital where Meryl seems to work as a surgical nurse. Nevertheless, Truman no longer trusts anyone except himself, since he has learned that appearances are deceptive.

Finally, his life seems to be totally confused when, most peculiarly, his father turns up after being believed dead for 22 years. What he "thought was a life begins to look like a lie [... and what he ...] thought was the world begins to look like a cage".[194]

---

[192] Rogerson referring to William Shakespeare's *As You Like It*, II.vii.139, 37

[193] With Truman being the only 'true' human being around the island, the minor-role players resemble the 'aliens' of Don Siegel's *Invasion of the Body Snatchers* (and its remakes). Similar to the infected people who have become mere human pods without emotions and desires, the minor-role players' behaviour does not correspond to the normal reactions of real people. This most prominent intertextual link within the film (which is evoked again when the cast constitute a search party and frisk the entire film universe in a concerted manhunt to prevent him from escaping) allows for a reading of *The Truman Show* as postmodern version of the *Body Snatchers*, in which Truman appears to be the only individual that rebels against the surface reality of the hyperreal world.

[194] Ken Sanes, *The Truman Show*. http://www.transparencynow.com/truman.htm (9 August 2010)

Agency panic

As Truman gradually comprehends that the people around him are not honest with him, he undertakes several attempts to break free from the place he is tied to by a dramaturgical traumatic childhood experience (his father's death by drowning). He must, however, realize that his discretionary powers are almost totally restricted.

Truman is not only denied access to information, for example when he attempts to contact his father, but is hindered by a group of marathon runners and the sudden kidnapping of his father, or when the security staff throws him out of the building where he had caught a visible glimpse of the truth. As controlling agents, the cast provide the necessary obstacles to prevent the protagonist's various attempts to escape.

When Truman tries to book a flight to the Fiji Islands (where he hopes to find Sylvia) the travel agency does not have any available, and when he wants to take the bus to Chicago the journey is cancelled. Truman finally takes his fake wife hostage, in order to escape by car, only to find the street he wants to drive along blocked by a sudden heavy traffic jam. When after a few minutes the same street appears to be completely deserted he knows that somebody does not want him to leave Seahaven.

Eventually managing to cross the bridge with Meryl's forced help, he ignores the fire warning only to be stopped at a road block due to an accident at the nuclear power station. Desperate and continually finding himself contained in an impasse, Truman breaks out of the car and tries to get away on foot. As he is outnumbered by the security staff around the restricted area it does not take them long to catch him. He is finally taken back 'home' by two policemen and received by a worried Meryl who tells him to visit a psychiatrist.

Truman's scopophobic visual paranoia thus accumulates into what Melley has termed 'agency panic'. Feeling that he is lost in somebody else's game, he 'suffers' from a loss of self-control over his own actions and intentions.[195]

The protagonist escapes the script

With all his attempts to escape ending in failure, Truman finally comes to the conclusion that the only possible way to escape his situation is to beat them at their own game. He therefore needs to subvert the system of his surrounding world by consciously becoming an element of the plot - both the narrative and the conspiracy - with his own secret plan.

---

[195] For 'agency panic' see Melley, 7-15

Truman secretly turns into an actor himself to satisfy the visual expectations of both the voyeuristic and the panoptic gaze. By pretending to be the old Truman he convinces them of the semblance of re-established order and control. He is, however, merely playing the role of the character he is supposed to be. Hiding his true intentions beneath the surface of his performance, he works out a strategy to escape.

Paradoxically, Truman has to accept the (fake) reality of the simulacrum and participate, by becoming a simulation of himself and another false sign in this hyperreal narrative. Adopting a false appearance finally enables him to become the true man he really is.[196]

The 'prisoner' finally tricks the empty panoptic gaze of the camera by replacing himself with a superficial fake appearance, a 'simulation' of himself being asleep. And when Christof's assistant blunders by not paying attention to the surveillance monitor he manages secretly to move out of the camera's reach. Thus, by deceiving 'their' gaze Truman finally escapes from the trap of visibility and disappears into the darkness of the huge panopticon at night.

At the end of both Christof's and Weir's narrative, Truman, having overcome the "clever bit of psychological programming", persistently moves closer to the frontier of his false existence.[197] When the foremast of his sailing boat pierces through the studio wall that is painted to resemble the sky and the god-like invisible voice from above finally confirms the worst paranoid assumptions about his existence, Truman's illusion of life is shattered completely.

When Truman climbs up the stairs and exits through the door of the wall that is covered with a celestial scene, he drops out of the narrative of his remote-controlled life. It is like a chick hatching out of the shell of the dome to be born again and explore the world outside the film universe. Thus, at the end of this *"Bildungsspiel* in a bubble" the overgrown child turns into a true man.[198] The hero of this spectacle in a dual sense, he finally becomes the adventurer he had always longed to be, bravely facing the challenges of an unknown reality in the world outside. Alluding to the Christian belief in eternal life, Truman, in leaving behind his false

---

[196] In this respect, it might be argued that his strategy functions according to the principles of second-stage simulation. The surface appearance of his acting ('everyday is wonderful!') conceals the true reality hidden beneath it: his wish to escape.

[197] Ken Sanes, *The Truman Show.* http://www.transparencynow.com/truman.htm (9 August 2010)

[198] O'Donnell, 4

personality, passes from the simulacrum to a true existence of an authentic life in the real world.[199]

If, however, the film's ending is read "as intentionally offering only the flimsiest of exits to Truman from an increasingly flimsy simulation", the conclusion of this visual game might be the conjecture that there is no end to his visual paranoia.[200] This 'open closure' might then be entertaining the suspicion that Truman only leaves *The Truman Show* to enter the next 'television-world' in which a different programme simulates another false reality; or it might even allude to "the possibility that everything is appearance, [and] that the world itself might be nothing but an elaborately staged fiction".[201]

Finally, on the meta-level, Truman's departure can be read as the ironic self-reflexive closure of a postmodern (cinematic) text. Even if he escapes Christof's clutches, Truman will never be free from the subjugation of a narrative that is someone else's fiction, because of his status as an element in a signifying chain.

4. The constructedness of postmodern reality

Truman as postmodern voyeur

The Truman Show is a postmodern horror tale. Disguised as a 'documentary drama', it presents a life that does not merely look suspiciously like but actually is a TV series. Michael Kokonis therefore points out that the film "pushes the epistemological commitment to cognitive values (Truman's search for existential knowledge) to the ontological issue of world making and unmaking".[202] As Truman resembles the human individual who finds himself lost in the simulated reality of a television show, the film depicts

---

[199] Ken Sanes mentions the biblical implications of *The Truman Show*. He identifies Truman with both Adam escaping from a false paradise and, by choice, falling into nature and history, and with Christ, in knowledge of a higher world, being crucified and resurrected to enter the sphere of heaven. Ken Sanes, *The Truman Show*. http://www.transparencynow.com/truman.htm (9 August 2010). Rogerson also reads the film as implying Christian allusions. She describes Truman as a secular Everyman who must overcome his own fear and the obstacles put in his way to be, in the face of death, stripped of everything he thought was his life (world) in order to pass over into a new life, determined to "face the realities of the unknown beyond the unreality" of the Seahaven film studios. Rogerson, 25

[200] O'Donnell, 4

[201] Romney, 40

[202] Kokonis, 58

the "reign of the hyperreal as [the] major symptom [of] and simultaneously contributing cause to the postmodern moment".[203]

Unlike Hitchcock's and Antonioni's photographers, neither a voyeur by profession nor initially searching for the truth, the protagonist of *The Truman Show* appears to be the incarnation of the postmodern voyeur in Denzin's sense. Truman does not deal with murder - he does not merely detect covert or immoral activities. His visual paranoia is of a more existential, all-embracing nature, since he is confronted with 'the agony of the real' (Baudrillard). An *'Everyman* of the Nineties' (Rogerson), he personifies Denzin's 'ordinary type', who learns the secret truth about the postmodern: that it is an age of simulated realities and hyperreality in which the truth 'masquerades as a fiction'. His scopophobic paranoia makes him realize that "the normal order of things itself amounts to a [media-based] conspiracy".[204] As Truman discovers that he can no longer trust what he sees, his visual investigation unmasks the truth of the simulacrum.[205]

A postmodern spectacle

The Truman Show explores the postmodern loss of the real on different narrative levels. The film can be read as an allegory of a postmodern media-dominated visual consumer culture, in which the boundaries between life and entertainment are blurred by the intermingling of life and the media.[206]

Through the on-screen audience, the 'real' people in *The Truman Show* are presented as mere spectators. They represent a society of the spectacle, a society in which voyeurism has established itself as mode of perception.

Glued to their TV sets, they consume Truman's life as a 'commodity-experience',[207] the show as representation of an alleged real life that substitutes their own authentic experiences.[208] When they gather in front of their TV screens, constituting a worldwide virtual televisual community,

---

[203] Kokonis, 57

[204] Knight, 3

[205] See Denzin, *Images of Postmodern Society* on the voyeur as postmodern 'seeker of truth', 155-156

[206] Baudrillard points out in *Simulations* (1983) that contemporary viewing follows the principles of "the dissolution of TV into life [... and ...] the dissolution of life into TV", as quoted in Friedberg, 136

[207] Friedberg (referring to Marx's "Theories of Surplus Value"), 54-55; for the commercialization of Truman's life, which reflects the on-screen audience's commercialization of life see O'Donnell, 7; Debord also points out that the spectacle promotes a materialized view of the world. Debord, 14

[208] See Debord, 13

they also find fulfilment of their desire for centredness, transparency and control in their otherwise decentred postmodern lives by concentrating their lives on *The Truman Show*.[209]

A nostalgic spectacle

As already mentioned, *The Truman Show* also touches on the Jamesonian definition of the nostalgia film.[210] With the setting located in a 1950s pastiche, Truman's world resembles the early days of television. The show, however, does not actually recreate this period. It rather quotes the style of the 1950s. Truman's favourite TV show *I Love Lucy* (a 1950s sitcom), the actor's clothing and the hints at president Truman are the symbolic ingredients by which this particular period is recognized, and which merely serve to reproduce its atmosphere.[211]

In consuming the 'glossy images of the past' the on-screen audience represents the inability of a postmodern society to 'map' its own present.[212] Instead it satisfies its nostalgic yearning with "pop images which simultaneously mock the past and the present".[213] The perverted picture of a superficially 'revisited' past contributes to the distortion of the representation of reality and thus to the postmodern notion of reality itself.

In this respect, *The Truman Show* also depicts the postmodern loss of historicity. While in Truman's case, isolation from the real world and the repetitiveness and predictability of his soap opera existence evokes a permanent present, the consumption of his life has become a compensatory substitute for the on-screen audience's loss of historicity.[214]

---

[209] O'Donnell, 7

[210] In Jameson's terms the film belongs to the third category of "films that are set in the present but invoke the past. [... Weir's ...] film's narrative and its art direction [Christof's TV show] confuse its sense of temporality". (The latter contributes to the film's reflection of the postmodern loss of historicity.) Friedberg (referring to Jameson and the nostalgia film), 168

[211] Peter and Will Brooker, eds. *Postmodern After-Images. A Reader in Film, Television and Video* (London and New York: Arnold, 1997), 5, 21. (Romney also points out a nostalgia for film-making practices of the past, "for an age in which the all-powerful auteur actually created things in real time and space, film sets as big as the world they portrayed". Romney, 42)

[212] Jameson points out an incapability of dealing with time and history as symptomatic of postmodern society. He describes the nostalgia narrative (and the use of pastiche) as an expression of this inability. See Fredric Jameson, *Nostalgia for the Present*, as referred to in Friedberg 168-169, 188

[213] See also Denzin, *Cinematic Society*, 46

[214] O'Donnell, 5

Finally, the spectators of the show represent a society that expresses a desire for consumption of a world merely consisting of images of itself and pseudo events and spectacles. In this respect, *The Truman Show* can be read as an ironic critical comment on the logic of late capitalism.[215]

In the end, the on-screen audience is not much better off than Truman. It, too, is separated from reality by the media-simulated images that it accepts as real. Its gaze is also deceived, and the distorted reality presented to it also creates a false consciousness.[216] It is therefore just as much a captive of *The Truman Show* as Truman himself, and, accordingly, it is as prone to being manipulated as he is.[217]

The postmodern as panoptic order

The intricate network of hidden cameras all around Seahaven alludes to the interconnectedness of the postmodern globalized world based on the images of media technology and their omnipresence. Kokonis, therefore, points out that *The Truman Show* might be read as the obverse of Hitchcock's "quasi or covert metafiction" of *Rear Window*. Whereas the latter "marked the transition from modernism to postmodernism by foregrounding its ontological questions through the device of the returned gaze [...] that shattered the 'fourth wall' of conventional theatricality", Weir's film functions "as a (metafictional) allegory of the power of the virtual gaze, effected by (new) cinematic and televisual apparatuses".[218]

Finally, *The Truman Show* is (a) "multi-level ontological allegory of the power of the media".[219] As an expression of cultural paranoia the film articulates the worries of a society whose culture and pervasive concept of reality has come to rely to a great extent on the visual and, in particular, the images provided by the media.

Visual paranoia in *The Truman Show* thus reflects the anxiety of being exposed to manipulation and domination. This includes a feeling of uneasiness about the intrusion into the private sphere by a cinematic-

---

[215] See Fredric Jameson, "Zur Logik der Kultur im Spätkapitalismus" in *Postmoderne. Zeichen eines kulturellen Wandels*, eds. Andreas Huyssen and Klaus R. Scherpe (Reinbek bei Hamburg: Rowohlt, 1986), 63

[216] With reference to Baudrillard's elaborations on Disneyland it might be argued that for the on-screen audience the show exists to cover up the fact that outside the film universe things are not much different. They are supposed to believe that their lives are truly real. See Jean Baudrillard (*Simulations*, 1983) as quoted in Christopher Butler, *Postmodernism - A Very Short Introduction* (Oxford: University Press, 2002), 112-113

[217] See Debord, 14

[218] Kokonis, 61

[219] Kokonis, 65

panoptic gaze using advanced technological tools as instruments of surveillance and control. Both aspects also reflect the anxiety about a totalitarian conformity in this media-infiltrated society.

5. The scopophobic paranoia plot in *The Truman Show*

Truman Burbank initially lives in a panoptic world. Almost every moment of his life is captured by the 5000 cameras in Seahaven and transmitted to the audience around the world.

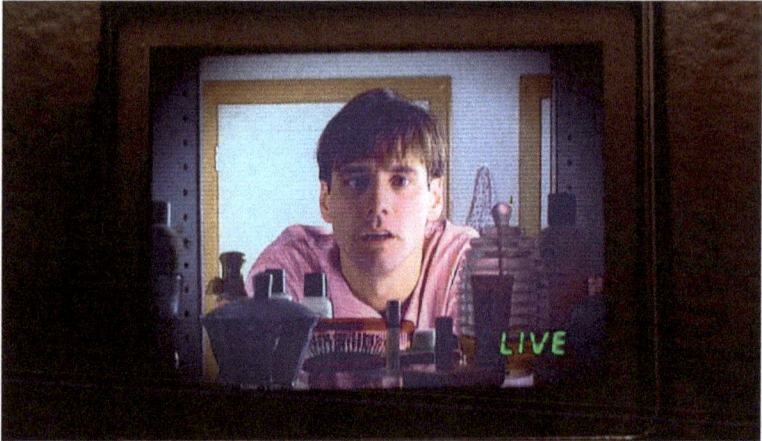

Truman's everyday morning ritual: looking into the Spanish mirror and talking to himself.

On his way to work the cameras never lose sight of Truman, switching from one perspective to the next.

The uninterrupted network of cameras resembles a modern monitoring system: closed-circuit television. The cameras surreptitiously trace Truman's every step.

'Normal' video surveillance is integrated into the network of cameras hunting Truman.

Truman is recorded from even the most ludicrous angle, such as, for example, the shot from the electric pencil sharpener (or 'button shots' from his counterparts' clothes).

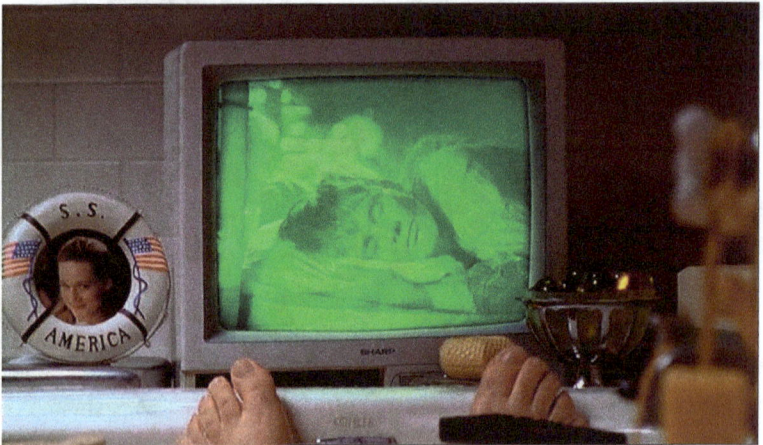

And even when he sleeps at night Truman is on air. He cannot escape the 'public eye'.

However, not only is video control omnipresent, the video surveillance of Truman's life is supplemented by the 'agent-actors' nearby, who play the counterparts and extras of Truman's life. They observe Truman's every step out of the corner of their eyes. Connected to the control room of the panoptic camera system they are ready to report whenever something unplanned and objectionable happens. And they are immediately on the spot to induce selective corrective measures to subdue the situation.

In the past, there had been a leak in the system that becomes the root of all doubt: as a young man Truman is attracted by a pretty actress who feels sympathy for him and tells him that he is in a show and that everything around him is not real. With her 'meta-knowledge' she tries to circumvent diverse cameras and escape into the shade of their dead angles to direct him to the sea – the supposedly natural border of his freedom.

Soon after the hasty attempt, the 'schizophrenic' girl is taken away from 'her father' and is completely removed from the show, that is, Truman's life. Truman is told that she has moved to Fiji, which initiates a strong yearning in him to leave Seahaven and find her.

The first sign that Truman's life is getting out of control: one morning, a lamp falling from the sky unsettles the everyday ritualized ceremony.

Truman can make neither head nor tails of that incident. A few minutes later, the radio presenter will explain that it belongs to an aeroplane that is said to have had an accident.

The next sign: When Truman disputes his own fate a sudden storm urges him to go home. However, the rain behaves like a silly shower, hunting him. Truman's initial incredulousness is followed by amusement - given the rain is falling just on him.

Another strange occurrence: A homeless man, resembling Truman's father, crosses Truman's path. Truman is stunned. He lost his father as a seven year old boy when their ship got into distress at sea and capsized.

The next clue: The frequency on which stage directions are transmitted to the actors populating the Seahaven setting gets accidentally tangled up with the radio programme Truman is listening to on his way to work. He suddenly realizes that the voice is tracking his every move.

When they realize that Truman has noticed their goings-on, life in Seahaven comes to a standstill for a moment. The change of radio frequency to 'normal' causes everybody to stop for a second. Immediately afterwards, this incident is explained with the lame excuse that for a moment he had inadvertently heard the police radio.

The film staff is not prepared for Truman's doubtful deviations, since the standard programme does not add up anymore. Truman's irregular behaviour complicates an unobstructed course of action and challenges the improvisation skills of the extras:

When he unexpectedly enters the building next to his work place, the staff works up a sweat. They do not succeed in keeping him from discovering the 'real' catering behind the fake lift:

Truman suspects that he is the focus of attention of the people around him. Everybody is prepared for him, and always taking care of him. No bus or car will ever harm him.

... as long as he does not want to cross the borders of his habitual life. Signs of the false image of the world around Truman: bus, bus driver and passengers are merely extras and neither prepared nor allowed to act in a 'Truman leaves Seahaven' scene. The crowd leaves the bus like a fleeing mute flock of sheep, since the bus driver cannot drive the vehicle. The bus driver personally apologizes to Truman, who sadly and disappointedly remains seated.

Now that Truman knows that he seems to be in the focus of everybody's attention he behaves differently. When he sees his friend Marlon at work in a little shop he speaks to him about his suspicion in a whispered voice to avoid unwanted witnesses.

At odds with himself, somewhere between desperation and megalomania, he plays the fool for omnipresent public attention and tests the other apparent customers in the shop by freaking out (clapping hands or shouting like a lunatic), in order to see their reaction. The result is: they do not care, do not even look, and this seems very odd to Truman.

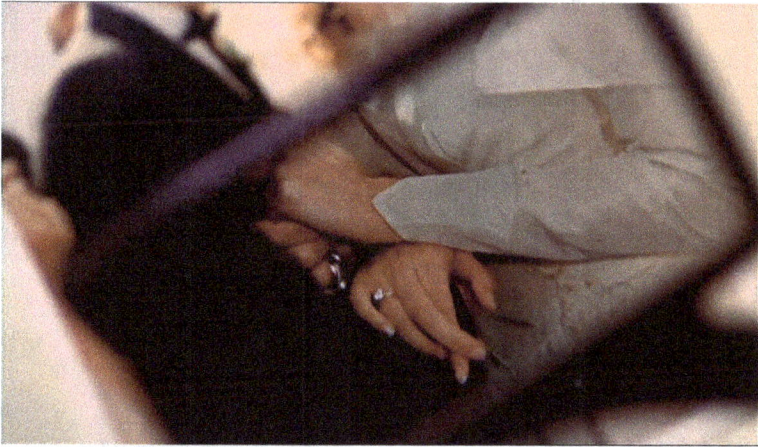

Truman cannot even rely on his wife, who is rattling off commercial propaganda instead of sticking with him no matter what happens. Whenever things get difficult she tries to escape his queries. One day he discovers her crossed fingers on their wedding picture: another visible sign for something going on behind the scenes.

Truman turns detective: He starts spying on his wife and follows her 'unseen' to the hospital where she 'works' as she hurries to get away from him after she has risked her neck with careless talk, desperately linking current events with the 'accident in the lift'.
In the hospital setting the team only just manages to make Truman believe in what they scramble to put across, namely everyday working life in a hospital.

With an uneasy sense of not only being the focus of events in Seahaven, but also of being surrounded by the marionettes of a system that wants to keep him in check, Truman puts the system to a test.

When Meril returns home from work Truman challenges her. He forces her to get into the car and locks the doors to avoid her escaping or talking her way out of everything. Together they track the artificial loop of the 'flowers', the 'bicycle' and the 'beetle' in the background. He has figured out the constant repetitive action of the extras, circling around or going to and fro by sitting in his car and secretly monitoring the surrounding area through the rear-view mirror.

Moreover, he forces Meril to go on a car trip with him, and prognosticates what will happen. And he is right! Everything comes to pass as he assumed: a traffic jam immediately occurs out of nothing to prevent him from breaking out...

...only to disappear again within a few seconds as soon as he has turned his back. He has outsmarted the sluggish system and figured out how it works.

The final straw: After Truman has managed to break through and cross the Seahaven bridge by car they meet the next obstacle, an accident at a nuclear power plant. However, what perplexes Truman the most is how it can be that the officer, who is unknown to him, knows his name?

In sheer horror, he jumps out of the car and runs for his life. The would-be employees of the nuclear facility chase after him with their 'camera-weapons' and finally manage to trap and tranquilize him, in order to take him home.

The last clue profoundly convinces Truman that Meril must be part of the game. By asking the staff in the control room to help her out when Truman attacks her (reminiscent of Lisa calling for Jeff's help when Thorwald has her in a headlock) she betrays herself. Truman knows that this is not a normal cry for help, and that somebody is watching them.

Finally, Truman outsmarts the system and beats it at its own game: In order to lull his visual controllers into a false sense of security, he gives them what they want, namely, the feeling that they have regained control over his life and actions.

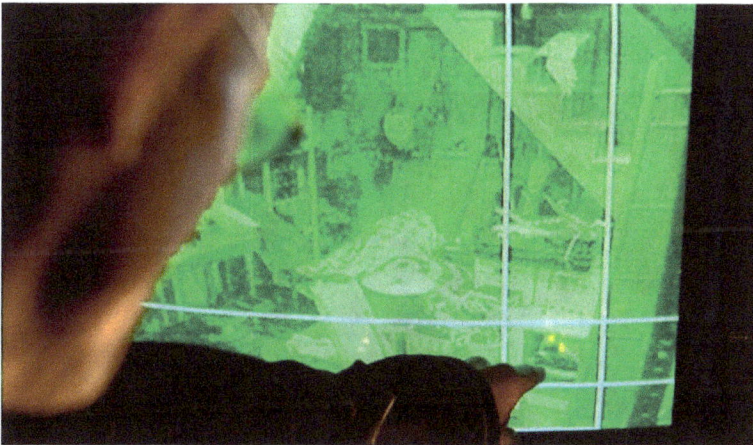

However, Christof, Truman's 'producer' cannot be fooled. He searches the documented material of the last few hours and finds the leak in Truman's demonstration of withdrawal and retreat into the basement.[220]

---

[220] This is the point at which the surveillance image can be characterized, according to Pauleit, as the photographesomenon. The mechanical gaze of the surveillance camera is at this moment not of the present time. It is enlivened through subsequent analysis and evaluation. Insofar as this panoptic gaze anticipates a future (*futur antérieur*), in which it has already passed, it becomes a second reality, security for unforeseen anomalies. See Pauleit, http://www.nachdemfilm.de/content/no-3-video-und-überwachung

Reminiscent of several 'Body Snatcher' films, the Seahaven troops march through the night to trace the 'deserter'.

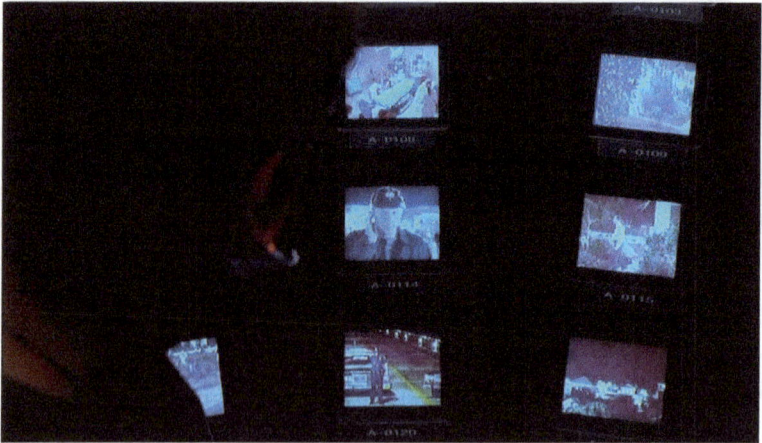

In the control room, the threads are coming together. All Seahaven can be kept under surveillance via a modern/postmodern panoptic video monitoring system.

The end of the lie (the simulacrum):

After Truman has survived the storm that he had to experience as Christof's revenge for his venturing into independence, he finally and literally reaches the limit of his so-called life. Crossing this last boundary he reaches his own, real life.

CONCLUSION

The films discussed in this book can be read as texts symbolic of postmodern culture. They reflect visual culture's focus on the spectacle. As "visual game[s] catering to the libidinal satisfaction of the sensory organ that postmodernity has deemed with ultimate importance, the eye", they simultaneously trace and indicate, as a concomitant of the postmodern condition a specific form of cultural paranoia: visual paranoia. [221]

Attempting to fathom reality the protagonist's of the films explore, as postmodern voyeur-detectives, the nature of the visual in a culture that, on the one hand, is increasingly dominated by visuality and, on the other, by a loss of the real.

It can also be argued that in the chronology of their release the films reflect a development towards visual culture's epistemological crisis of interpretation in an age of the hyperreal. Typical for the paranoia film, the protagonists' visual investigations of reality and its representations (or simulations) lead them to counter the seemingly obvious versions of reality with alternative interpretations. The initial realization of the ambiguity of visual appearances finally leads to the unmasking of the simulacrum.

Rear Window marks the first stage of this development. The scopophilic protagonist is a representative of a society that relies on visual perceptions as the main source of their assumptions about reality. Jeffries, however, gradually begins to question the reliability of surface appearances. He therefore scrutinizes his environment thoroughly with the help of his optical tools. The manner in which he reads the visual appearances as signs that confront him while solving a mystery, which turns out to be a crime, can be described as both postmodern and 'paranoid'.

As the film's closure provides a verification of the protagonist's suspicion and investigative visual perceptions, *Rear Window* can still claim "that the image can be matched to a firm object in the real world".[222] In this respect, Jeffries's visual paranoia is still concerned with the deceptive nature of visual appearances in general.

A further aspect of *Rear Window*, which also must be mentioned at this point, is the anticipation of the entrance of the spectacle into real life and thus postmodern blurring of boundaries - a characteristic which becomes clearer in *The Truman Show*.

The next stage of this development can be seen in *Blow-Up, which* is concerned with the representation of reality. Antonioni's photographer is

---

[221] Kokonis (referring to *The Truman Show*), 61

[222] Denzin, *Cinematic Society*, 137

an example of a member of a society who has increasingly come to rely on visual representations of reality. As he tries to fathom this reality with his camera, he discovers that his photographic representations, though reflecting reality, are signs to be interpreted, and that their meaning is relative. Although his blow-ups first help the protagonist to detect the hidden truth behind a superficial reality by revealing to him more than he saw with his own eyes, it becomes impossible for him to definitively verify his suspicions with their help. When they lack the most important element in the context of their significance - their referent - the images become simulacra. *Blow-Up* finds its conclusion in the statement that the law that "connects the image to its referent is finally dead".[223]

Finally, in *The Truman Show* this development culminates in the protagonist's scopophobic paranoia. He not only discovers the ambiguity of visual appearances, he also unmasks his world as a hyperreality, a reality which is completely lost in fake and empty images. It is a media-made construct consisting of simulacra created to betray his visual perception and control him. Truman discovers that not only his gaze has been deceived, he has also been trapped by the panoptic gaze hidden behind the simulation.

These three films thus trace the phenomenon of visual paranoia as a growing anxiety within a world in which visual perception seems to be the only existent reality. Paradoxically, this world is increasingly reliant on the images provided by the media.

As it has become difficult to differentiate between fake and real, between representations and simulations in the postmodern age, visual paranoia expresses the fundamental suspicion that seeing might no longer be believing, Within this culture what is perceived as real can turn out to be a distorted, masked reality or even a reality that has been replaced by a reality of the image. It therefore raises the question of who is in control of the images and decides about how reality is presented or represented.

Visual paranoia, however, is not merely an expression of scepticism regarding visual appearances. While both *Rear Window* and *Blow-Up* announced the end of privacy in the early postmodern age, *The Truman Show* developed the postmodern into a panoptic order, in which the private sphere is absorbed by the public sphere through the use of new cinematic apparatuses and visual technology.[224] These serve not merely to construct and manipulate the images of reality they produce, but also to survey and control those to whom these are presented. At this level, visual paranoia coincides with Melley's 'agency panic'. Those in control of the content of

---

[223] Denzin, *Cinematic Society,* 137

[224] Denzin, *Cinematic Society,* 137

images have the power to manipulate the society of the spectacle according to their requirements.

Finally, it remains to be said that all three films depict the postmodern world as one consisting of visual signs to be read. As visual paranoia leads the protagonists to doubt the former appearance of reality, their visual investigations conclude with the discovery that there is no objective reality. It always depends on one's perspective and the context, whether an interpretation of visual perceptions - concerning both reality and representations - will be regarded as paranoid or not. It is therefore also not possible to represent reality in just one appropriate way.

This aspect is reflected by the films' focus on visuality and their self-reflexive structures, with which they also incorporate the audience into this visual game. It is not so much life that constitutes the frame of reference for them, but rather the medial experience. In this way the audience(s) are made aware of the fact that any vision of reality, cinematic or otherwise, is always a construction.

Just as it has become difficult, if not impossible, to claim that there is one valid version of truth, in this postmodern age of visual culture there are countless possible ways to read and interpret the signs. Maybe we just have to be a little paranoid to catch a glimpse of reality...?

BIBLIOGRAPHY

Allen, Robert C. and Gomery, Douglas, eds. *Film History. Theory and Practice.* New York: McGraw-Hill, 1985

Alleva, Richard, "Two kinds of paranoia: *The Truman Show* and *The X-Files*" *Commonweal* August 14, 1998 http://www.thefreelibrary.com /Two+kinds+of+paranoia%3a+The+Truman+Show'+and+'The+X-Files.'+(motion...- a021058771 (10 August 2010)

Ansohn, Berthold, "Realitätserschütterung. Überlegungen zu Selbstreferenzialität und Realitätsverlust des Unterhaltungsfilms am Beispiel des Horrorfilms" in *medien praktisch* No. 1: *Auf der Suche nach der Wirklichkeit* (1996), 25-28

Balzer, Andreas, "Der verdunkelte Horizont" in *Grimme. Zeitschrift für Programm, Forschung und Medienproduktion* No. 3 (1998), 52-53

Barry, Peter, *Beginning Theory. An Introduction to Literary and Cultural Theory.* Manchester and New York: Manchester University Press, 1995

Bauman, Zygmunt, *Unbehagen in der Postmoderne.* Hamburg: Hamburger Edition, 1999

Belton, John, ed. *Alfred Hitchcock's 'Rear Window'.* Cambridge, UK: University Press, 2000.

Binotto, Thomas, "The Peter Weir Show. Wir sind in dieser Welt nie wirklich zu Hause" in *Zoom* No. 11 (1998), 12-22

Boyd, David, "Images of Interpretation: *Blow-Up*" in *Film and the Interpretive Process. A Study of 'Blow-Up', 'Rashomon', 'Citizen Kane', '81/2', 'Vertigo' and 'Persona'.* (New York, Bern, Frankfurt am Main, Paris: Peter Lang, 1989), 19-49

Bozovic, Miran, "The Man Behind His Own Retina" in *Everything You Always Wanted to Know about Lacan (but were Afraid to Ask Hitchcock).* Ed. Slavoj Zizek. (London, New York: Verso, 1992), 161-177

Braudy, Leo, *The World in a Frame: What We See in Films.* Chicago and London: Chicago University Press, 2002

Braudy, Leo and Cohen, Marshall, eds. *Film Theory and Criticism. Introductory Readings.* New York and Oxford: Oxford University Press, 1999

Brooker, Peter and Will, eds. *Postmodern After-Images. A Reader in Film, Television and Video.* London and New York: Arnold, 1997

Brunette, Peter, "*Blow-Up* (1966)" in *The Films of Michelangelo Antonioni.* (New York: Cambridge University Press, 1998), 109-126

Bühler, Gerhard, *Postmoderne auf dem Bildschirm, auf der Leinwand: Musikvideos, Werbespots und David Lynchs 'Wild at Heart'.* St. Augustin: Gardez, 2002

Bürger, Peter, *Ursprung des postmodernen Denkens.* Weilerswist: Velbrück Wissenschaft, 2000

Butler, Christopher, *Postmodernism - A Very Short Introduction.* Oxford: University Press, 2002

Chatman, Seymour, "*Il provino* and *Blow-Up*" in *Antonioni or The Surface of the World.* (Berkeley, Los Angeles, London: UCP, 1985), 136-158

Colier, F., *These Memories Can Wait.* http://www.altered-ego.net/ ART%20Films/memento.htm. (18 July 2010)

Debord, Guy, *Die Gesellschaft des Spektakels*. Berlin: Verlag Klaus Bittermann, 1996

Degli-Esposti, Cristina, ed. *Postmodernism in The Cinema* (papers from a conference held in 1994 at Kent State University) Kent, Ohio: Berghahn Books, 1998

Denzin, Norman K., *Images of Postmodern Society: Social Theory and Contemporary Cinema*. London, Newbury Park and New Delhi: Sage Publications, 1991

The Cinematic Society. The Voyeur's Gaze. London, Thousand Oaks, New Delhi: Sage Publications, 1995

Desalm, Brigitte, "Überwachen und Strafen - Einiges über die Blicke bei Hitchcock" in *Alfred Hitchcock*. Eds. Lars-Olav Beier and Georg Seeßlen. (Berlin: Bertz, 1999), 39-56

Docherty, Thomas, ed. *Postmodernism. A Reader*. New York: Pearson Education, 2003

Dolar, Mladen, "A Father Who Is Not Quite Dead" in *Everything You Always Wanted to Know about Lacan (but were Afraid to Ask Hitchcock)*. Ed. Slavoj Zizek. (London, New York: Verso, 1992), 143-150

du, *Special Issue on Michelangelo Antonioni*, No. 11 (November 1995)

Eberwein, Robert T., "The Master Text of *Blow-Up*" in *Close Viewings*. Ed. Peter Lehman. (Tallahassee: Florida State University Press, 1990), 262-281

Eder, Jens, ed. *Oberflächenrausch. Postmoderne und Postklassik im Kino der 90er Jahre*. Münster, Hamburg, London: Lit-Verlag, 2002

Everschor, Franz, "The Truman Show" in *film-dienst* 23 (1998) [quoted in *Lexikon des internationalen Films 2000/2001* (CD-ROM) München: Net World Vision GmbH, 2000.]

Faßler, Manfred, *Bildlichkeit - Navigationen durch das Repertoire der Sichtbarkeit*. Wien, Köln, Weimar: Böhlau, 2002

Faulstich, Werner, *Die Filminterpretation*. Göttingen: Vandenhoeck und Ruprecht, 1988

Felix, Jürgen, ed. *Die Postmoderne im Kino: Ein Reader*. Marburg: Schüren, 2002

Felix, Jürgen et al., eds. "Filmische Selbstreflexionen" in *Augenblick. Marburger Hefte zur Medienwissenschaft* 31. Marburg: Schüren, 2000

Fenster, Mark, *Conspirary Theories. Secrecy and Power in American Culture*. Minneapolis, London: Minnesota University Press, 1999

Foster, Hal, ed. *Vision and Visuality*. (Dia Art Foundation, Discussions in Contemporary Culture No. 2). New York: The New Press, 1988/99

Foucault, Michel, *Überwachen und Strafen*. Frankfurt am Main: Suhrkamp, 1976

Fried, Yehuda and Agassi, Joseph, *Paranoia: A Study in Diagnosis*. Dordrecht, Boston: D. Reidel Publishing Company, 1976

Friedberg, Anne, *Window Shopping: Cinema and the Postmodern*. Berkeley, Los Angeles and Oxford: UCP, 1993

Gaggi, Silvio, *From Text to Hypertext: Decentering the Subject in Fiction, Film, the Visual Arts, and Electronic Media*. Philadelphia: Pennsylvania University Press, 1997.

Gardner, Colin, *Antonioni's Blow-Up and the Chiasmus of Memory*. http://www:artbrain.org/journal2/gardner.html. (25 July 2010)

Gerdes, Julia Margarita, "Blow-Up" in *Reclam Filmklassiker* Vol. 3 (1965-1981). Ed. Thomas Koebner. (Stuttgart: Reclam, 1995), 80-88

Hahn, Ronald M., and **Giesen**, Rolf, *Alfred Hitchcock. Der Meister der Angst*. München: Knaur, 1999

Hayward, Susan, *Cinema Studies: The Key Concepts*. New York and London: Routledge, 2000

Herwig, Jana, "Illusion, Simulation, Virtualität. Zur Modalität der medialen Wirklichkeiten von Kino, Fernsehen, World Wide Web" in *Mediale Wirklichkeiten (Film- und Fernsehwissenschaftliches Kolloquium* 15). Ed. Andrea Nolte. (Marburg: Schüren, 2003), 68-75.

Hickethier, Knut, *Film- und Fernsehanalyse*. Stuttgart, Weimar: J.B. Metzler, 1996

Hill, John, "Film and Postmodernism" in *Encyclopedia of Postmodernism*. Ed. Victor E. Taylor. (London: Routledge, 2001), 96-97

Hofstadter, Richard, *The Paranoid Style in American Politics and Other Essays*. New York: Alfred A. Knopf, 1965

Hutcheon, Linda, *A Poetics of Postmodernism. History, Theory, Fiction*. New York and London: Routledge, 1988

The Politics of Postmodernism. London and New York: Routledge, 2002

Huyssen, Andreas and **Scherpe**, Klaus R., eds. *Postmoderne. Zeichen eines kulturellen Wandels*. Reinbek bei Hamburg: Rowohlt, 1986

Jameson, Fredric, *Postmodernism or, The Cultural Logic of Late Capitalism*. London and New York: Verso, 1991

Kelly, Michael, "A Reporter at Large. The Road to Paranoia" in *The New Yorker* (19 June 1995), 60-69

Keutzer, Oliver, "Project Zweifel. Verdachtsmomente im Paranoia-Thriller" in *Kino der Extreme. Kulturanalytische Studien (Filmstudien Vol. 8)*. Ed. Marcus Stiglegger. St. Augustin: Gardez, 2002

Kirchman, Kay, "Zwischen Selbstreflexivität und Selbstreferenzialität. Überlegungen zur Ästhetil des Selbstbezüglichen als filmischer Modernität" in *Im Spiegelkabinett der Illusionen. Filme über sich selbst (Arnoldshainer Filmgespräche Vol. 13)*. Ed. Ernst Karpf et al. (Marburg: Schüren, 1996), 67-86

Kleinspehn, Thomas, *Der flüchtige Blick. Sehen und Identität in der Kultur der Neuzeit*. Reinbek bei Hamburg: Rowohlt, 1989

Knight, Peter, *Conspiracy Culture: From Kennedy to the X-Files*. London: Routledge, 2000

Kokonis, Michael, "Postmodernism, Hyperreality and the Hegemony of Spectacle in New Hollywood: The Case of *The Truman Show*" in *Gramma. Periodiko Theorias Kai Kritikes* No. 7 (Thessaloniki, 1999), 41-72

Lane, Anthony, "Look and Yearn. Peter Weir Creates a New World in *The Truman Show*" in *The New Yorker* (The Critics: Current Cinema, 15 June 1998), 80-81

Lerude-Flechet, Martine, "Schauspiel des Blicks" in *Das unbewusste Sehen: Texte zu Psychoanalyse, Film, Kino*. Gesellschaft für Filmtheorie. Eds. August Ruhs et al. (Wien: Löcker, 1989), 100-113

Levin, Thomas Y., "Die Rhetorik der Überwachung - Angst vor Beobachtung in den zeitgenössischen Medien" in *Nach dem Film* No 3: *Video und Überwachung* (1/10/2001); http://www.nachdemfilm.de/content/die-rhetorik-der-überwachung (14 August 2010)

Marcus, Greil, "A Dream of the Cold War: On *The Manchurian Candidate*" in *The Dustbin of History* (Cambridge Massachusetts: Harvard University Press, 1995), 192-207

McGregor, Peter, '*The Truman Show*' as a study of '*the Society of the Spectacle*'. Film As Text - Critical Essay. Published in *Australian Screen Education* | March 22, 2003 http://www.accessmylibrary.com/article-1G1-108551753/truman-show-study-society.html (14 August 2010)

Mc Hale, Brian, *Constructing Postmodernism*. London and New York: Routledge, 1992

McQuire, Scott, *Visions of Modernity: Representation, Memory, Time and Space in the Age of the Camera*. London, Thousand Oaks and New Delhi: Sage Publications, 1998

Melley, Timothy, *Empire of Conspiracy: The Culture of Paranoia in Postwar America*. Ithaca and London: Cornell University Press, 2000

Merker, Helmut, "Rear Window" in *Alfred Hitchcock*. Eds. Lars-Olav Beier and Georg Seeßlen. (Berlin: Bertz, 1999), 364-369

Metz, Christian, *Film Language: A Semiotics of the Cinema*. Chicago: University Press, 1991

Miller, Toby and Stam, Robert, eds. *A Companion to Film Theory*. Malden, Massachusetts and Oxford: Blackwell, 1999

Mirzoeff, Nicholas, *An Introduction to Visual Culture*. London and New York: Routledge, 1999

Morawski, Stefan, *The Troubles with Postmodernism*. New York: Routledge, 1996

Naziri, Gérard, *Paranoia im amerikanischen Kino. Die 70er Jahre und die Folgen. (Filmstudien Vol. 35)*. Sankt Augustin: Gardez, 2003

Neupert, Richard John, *The End: Narration and Closure in the Cinema*. Detroit, Michigan: Wayne State University Press, 1995

Nicol, Bran, "Reading Paranoia. Paranoia, Epistemophilia and the Postmodern Crisis of Interpretation" in *Literature and Psychology. A Journal of Psychoanalytic and Cultural Critics*, 45.1-2 (Nashville, Tennessee: MLA of America, 1999), 44-62

Noll Brinckmann, Christine, "Die filmische Urszene und der Film. Die Urszene" in *Das unbewusste Sehen: Texte zu Psychoanalyse, Film, Kino*. Gesellschaft für Filmtheorie. Eds. August Ruhs et al. (Wien: Löcker, 1989), 20-43

O'Donnell, Patrick, *Latent Destinies. Cultural Paranoia and Contemporary U.S. Narrative*. Durham and London: Duke University Press, 2000

Oppermann, Gerard, "Die Mittelszene des Filmes *Blow-Up*" in *Michelangelo Antonioni*. Eds. Jan Berg and Hans-Otto Hügel. (Hildesheim: Universität Hildesheim, Institut für Theater und Medienwissenschaft, 1995), 7-37

Pallasmaa, Juhani, *The Architecture of Image. Existential Space in Cinema*. Helsinki: Rakennustieto, 2001

Pauleit, Winfried, "Videoüberwachung und postmoderne Subjekte. Ein Hypertext zu den Facetten einer Bildmaschine" in *Nach dem Film* No 3: *Video und Überwachung* (1/10/2001); http://www.nachdemfilm.de/content/videoüberwachung-und-postmoderne-subjekte (14 August 2010)

"Videoüberwachung und die Condition Postmoderne" in *Ästhetik & Kommunikation* 106, (1999), 99-106

Pelko, Stojan, "Punctum Caecum, or, Of Insight and Blindness" in *Everything You Always Wanted to Know about Lacan (but were Afraid to Ask Hitchcock.)* Ed. Slavoj Zizek. (London, New York: Verso, 1992), 106-121

Pipes, Daniel, *Conspiracy. How the Paranoid Style Flourishes and Where It Comes from.* New York, London, Toronto, Sydney, Singapore: The Free Press, 1997

Pratt, Ray, *Projecting Paranoia. Conspiratorial Visions in American Film.* Lawrence: Kansas University Press, 2001

Reinecke, Stefan, "Wenn das Kino über sich selbst staunt" in *Im Spiegelkabinett der Illusionen. Filme über sich selbst (Arnoldshainer Filmgespräche Vol. 13).* Ed. Ernst Karpf, et al. (Marburg: Schüren, 1996), 9-15

Rogerson, Margaret, "The Truman Show: An *Everyman* for the Late 1990s" in *Sydney Studies in English,* No. 26 (Sydney, N.S.W., 2000), 25-44

Editors of **Rolling Stone,** *The Age of Paranoia. How the Sixties Ended.* New York: Pocket Book, 1972

Romney, Jonathan, "The New Paranoia - Paranoia of Images. Games Pixels Play" in *Film Comment* 34.6 (New York, Film Society of Lincoln Center, 1998), 39-43

Rost, Andreas, and **Sandbothe,** Mike, eds. *Die Filmgespenster der Postmoderne.* Frankfurt am Main: Verlag der Autoren, 1998.

Sachs-Hombach, Klaus, ed., Bildtheorien. *Anthropologische und kulturelle Grundlagen des Visualistic Turn.* Frankfurt am Main: Suhrkamp, 2009

Salje, Gunther, "Blow-Up" in *Antonioni. Regieanalyse, Regiepraxis.* (Bassum: Verlag Media-Institut, 1996), 203-227

Sanes, Ken, The Truman Show. http://www.transparencynow.com/truman.htm (09 August 2010)

Schäfer, Horst, and **Schwarzer,** Wolfgang, *Top Secret: Agenten- und Spionagefilme - Personen, Affären, Skandale.* Berlin: Henschel, 1998

Schmidt, Johann N., "Das Fenster zum Hof" in *Reclams Lexikon der Filmklassiker. (Beschreibungen und Kommentare)* Vol. 2 1947-1964. Ed. Thomas Koebner. (Stuttgart: Reclam, 1995), 205-209

Schröder, Nicolaus, *50 Klassiker Film. Die Wichtigsten Werke der Filmgeschichte.* Hildesheim: Gerstenberg, 2000

Scott, Ian, **American Politics in Hollywood Film.** Edinburgh: University Press, 2000

Seeßlen, Georg, *Kino der Angst: Grundlagen des populären Films.* Marburg: Schüren, 1995

Sentürk, Ritvan, **Postmoderne Tendenzen im Film** (Dissertation, 1998). Friedrich-Alexander-Universität Erlangen-Nürnberg, 1999.

Sharff, Stefan, *The Art of Looking in Hitchcock's Rear Window.* New York: Limelight Editions, 1997

Sim, Stuart, ed. *The Routledge Companion to Postmodernism*. London: Routledge, 2001

Skutski, Karl J. "A VIEWER'S GUIDE TO *BLOW-UP*" (prepared for the Department of Modern Languages and Literatures of Duquesne University in April 2008) http://www.skutski.org/blowupviewersguide.doc (14 August 2010)

Stoermer, Fabian, "Unschuldige Beweise. Michelangelo Antonioni, *Blow up*, Peter Greenaway, *Der Kontrakt des Zeichners*" in *Nach dem Film* No 8: *Fotokino* (1/12/2005);   http://www.nachdemfilm.de/content/unschuldige-beweise (14 August 2010)

Sturken, Marita and Cartwright, Lisa, *Practices of Looking: An Introduction to Visual Culture*. Oxford: University Press, 2001

Taylor, Henry M., "Was bleibt ist das Kino. Ein Gespenst der Filmgeschichte: auf den Spuren des Paranoia-Films" *Filmbulletin* 1 (2003), 45-51

Taylor, Victor E., ed. *Encyclopedia of Postmodernism*. London: Routledge, 2001

Töteberg, Michael, ed. *Metzler-Film-Lexikon*. Stuttgart, Weimar: Metzler, 1995

Vogel, Amos, *Film als subversive Kunst: Kino wieder die Tabus - von Eisenstein bis Kubrick*. Reinbek bei Hamburg: Rowohlt, 2000

Welsch, Wolfgang, ed. *Wege aus der Moderne. Schlüsseltexte der Postmoderne-Diskussion*. Berlin: Akademie, 1994

Winter, Rainer, *Filmsoziologie: Eine Einführung in das Verhältnis von Film, Kultur und Gesellschaft*. München: Quintessenz, 1992

Wood, Robin, *Hitchcock's Films*. London, New York: Zwemmer/Barnes, 1965

  Hitchcock's Films Revisited. London and Boston: Faber and Faber, 1989

Zizek, Slavoj, "Alfred Hitchcock, or, The Form and its Historical Mediation" in *Everything You Always Wanted to Know about Lacan (but were Afraid to Ask Hitchcock)*. Ed. Slavoj Zizek. London, New York: Verso, 1992

ibidem-Verlag

Melchiorstr. 15

D-70439 Stuttgart

info@ibidem-verlag.de

www.ibidem-verlag.de
www.ibidem.eu
www.edition-noema.de
www.autorenbetreuung.de

www.ingramcontent.com/pod-product-compliance
Lightning Source LLC
Chambersburg PA
CBHW062039270326
41929CB00014B/2475